Speak to me

Speak to me

Marcia
Calhoun
Forecki

Gallaudet College Press
Washington, D.C.

Gallaudet College Press
Washington, DC 20002

Published 1985
Printed in the United States of America

Library of Congress Cataloging in Publication Data

Forecki, Marcia Calhoun, 1951-
  Speak to me.

  1. Children, Deaf—Family relationships. 2.
Deaf—Education. I. Title.
HV2392.2.F67   1985   362.4'2'0924   84-28740
ISBN 0-913580-95-3

Gallaudet College is an equal opportunity employer/educational institution.
Programs and services offered by Gallaudet College receive substantial financial support from the U.S. Department of Education.

This book is for my family, who helped me through it;
For Judy, who made me write about it;
And for Charlie, so he may understand it.

Prologue

A cold Iowa Sunday afternoon. I sit on the floor with my son. We are playing with his collection of miniature cars. His collection rivals that of the Big Three and the houses of Nissan and Mitsubishi combined.

Today, we are driving up and down roads we've built of blocks. A noise in the parking lot draws my attention; the spinning of tires on ice. Some poor devil is trying to get up the hill. I leave the little cars on the floor and move to the window. I watch on tiptoe, looking over the level of frost growing on the inside of the glass. The driver makes one futile attempt at the hill, then two, three. Charlie is still playing with the cars on the floor. The sound of the spinning tires begins to grind on my nerves just as the rubber grinds itself into the unyielding ice. Charlie looks up and notices I am missing from the game. He comes to watch, too. I hold him up so he can see the fourth and final attempt to scale the driveway. The car rolls back, nearly invisible beneath the cloud of its exhaust smoke. Charlie looks at me and shrugs. I shrug in response.

Bored with the cars (I am, not he), I suggest a snack. Charlie seems agreeable and follows me to the portion of our living room held out as a kitchen. "What would you like?" I ask.

"Peanut butter," answers Charlie.

"All right. Peanut butter and crackers?"

"No."

"Peanut butter and toast?"

"Brown."

1

"Brown? Brown what?"

"Brown."

"Brown bread?"

"Brown."

"Brown what?"

"Brown."

"Show me." Charlie looks up at the open cabinet. He wears a searching expression as his eyes move from item to item.

"Brown."

"Brown what? How about these crackers?" I take out the box of saltines, but he shakes his head no.

What is brown that relates to peanut butter? Pancakes? A remote possibility, but worth a try. I hold out a box of pancake mix. "Do you want pancakes and peanut butter?"

Charlie shakes his head emphatically. "Brown." He is losing patience. I suggest other snack items, even to the extreme of cooking something. No, he wants something brown.

"Let's play with the cars." Even that is preferable to playing riddles about brown food.

Charlie's face becomes insistent. "Brown, brown." Charlie tries very hard to say it clearly. The *br* and *n* are missing, but the *ow* and the sign are unmistakable. He looks up at me and repeats *ow*, then signs, "Good speech."

"Yes, that's very good speech. Brown what?" I'm beginning to panic. Getting him to make such an effort to say a word usually requires all the persuasion, bribery, and praise I can muster. What in hell is there to eat with peanut butter that is brown?

Charlie is repeating the *ow*, holding his hand on his throat. He believes that if he can make a good sound, he'll get whatever it is he wants. If I can't come up with it, he may decide that speech is a waste of time and so he may never try to speak again. It is, after all, something he does strictly for the benefit of others. He gets little personal satisfaction from speaking. He can't even be sure he's said it correctly, or nominally so, unless someone else tells him he has. It's an effort for him and it's difficult. Without speech, he may grow up unable to live independently. He'll be cut off from the job market. He'll lose all confidence and wind up a hopeless pauper dependent on the public weal; or worse, dependent on me. He's only six now. I can't take his being dependent on me for another fifty or sixty years.

"Store," Charlie signs. I don't want to go out in the cold to a store to buy something brown. But, I must. Charlie's future seems to depend on it. Besides, if he thinks I don't understand him, he may grow up to hate me. The thought of his being dependent on me and hating me for another half-century is too much to bear.

"Put on your coat. We're going to the store. We'll buy brown."

Gleefully, Charlie turns toward the closet (located in another corner of the same living room) for his coat. I remember the ice-covered hill. Will the car make it down? Or back up again? We'll have to walk.

Boots, scarves, mittens for two. Fifteen minutes later, we're ready. I'm exhausted by now. Charlie is delighted.

"One car," he signs, using his imploring expression.

"No. I'm not buying any more cars. The brown and that's it. Let's go."

The hill is treacherous. I hold Charlie's mittened hand and turn my feet sideways for a better grip. Charlie lets go of my hand, pulls off his mitten, and signs, "Brown."

"I know," I try to say, but the howling wind pushes the words back down my throat. I nod vigorously as I shove the mitten back on his hand.

It's only a short block to the convenience store, but each step through the snow takes precious time. I can barely feel my feet. Charlie looks up at me, laughs, and signs something. It is hidden by the mitten, but I nod and pull him along. My arm is starting to ache from his pulling it back. I slow down to ease the pressure and he slows down accordingly. Will we ever get there?

Inside the store, I remove my mittens. "Where brown?" My fingers are stiff and the signs are clumsy. Charlie pulls me along. Up one aisle and down another, he scrutinizes the items on the shelves. I let him take his time, happy for the warmth of the store. My nose starts to run.

Charlie pulls away from my hand and runs to the end of an aisle, his boots flopping noisily. He stops short in front of boxes of graham crackers. "Brown," he says, pointing. Our mission's end. My mind scans back to other boxes of graham crackers bought for Charlie but thrown away after being ignored for months in the cabinet. His expression, though, makes this trip (somewhat) worthwhile. He repeats *ow*. It is high pitched and nasal, but he is as proud of his voice as is a coloratura. Motivation is what he needs to learn to speak, and I have managed to give him a bit of it. (Until the next time he says something I don't understand.) We pay for the graham crackers and begin the arduous trek home.

Meet my son. Six years, seven gray hairs, and a lifetime ago he was born. He has a face that could be described as angelic, if by that you mean perfect in form and innocent in expression. A shaggy scallop of brown wavy hair frames his creamy complexion. His hazel eyes are bright and wide enough to take in my slightest change of mood, my every weakness. He looks out at the world from beneath a triple fringe of eyelashes. His energy is boundless, with the regenerative power of a breeder reactor. On a few crackers and some peanut butter, he can maintain constant motion for a whole day and as far into the night as he can bargain. He is as perceptive as a good lawyer watching a jury. He knows the precise moment when my breaking point is imminent, and only then he pulls back and smiles through upturned eyes while holding up three fingers that mean *I love you*. Did I mention? Charlie is deaf.

1

"When did you discover your son was deaf?"

"When he was about a year and a half."

"You mean you lived with a child for a year and a half and didn't realize that he couldn't hear anything you said?"

"Well, you see, sometimes he seemed to respond. And, you know how children are at ignoring people when they want to. Sometimes, when I told him no, he would go right on with what he was doing; other times he would stop. He wasn't consistent, but he did seem to respond, sometimes."

"I see. How convenient for you. Tell me, did this sometimes responsive child make any sounds?"

"He said, 'M-m-m.' "

"Go on."

"That's it. Just 'M-m-m.' "

"No other sounds?"

"No."

"No 'Da-da,' for instance?"

"No."

"He made just this one sound until when?"

"Until always. Until we started teaching him as a deaf child. He makes other sounds now, but that was the only good sound until he was almost three."

"And that seemed normal to you?"

"Well, Charlie was my first child. I mean, well, of course, I had been around other children before, but not tiny infants. Not from birth. Not day in and day out."

"But you read books. Surely they gave you some idea of what to expect in the way of speech development."

"Well, yes. But, Charlie wasn't always on time with everything. He didn't get his first tooth until he was thirteen months old. Some children talk later than others. They save it up, or something. Remember the old story about the child who didn't talk for years? Never even tried to talk, no matter how her parents coaxed or tried to trick her. Then, one day, when she was five or six years old, her mother was putting on her shoes, and the little girl said to her mother, 'Too tight.' Her mother was ecstatic with joy. When the mother calmed down, she asked the little girl why she had never said anything before now. The girl answered, 'Until now, everything has been all right.'"

"You expected Charlie to break out in Hamlet's soliloquy one day? When he was ready? Is that right?"

"Something like that."

"More likely he would have said, 'Hey, stupid! I can't hear.'"

"I would have been delighted if he had."

This conversation has never actually taken place. It's a dream (read nightmare) I've had for several years. I go through the whole conversation, taking both parts, every time I look into what I perceive to be a pair of accusing eyes when I say I discovered Charlie's deafness at age one-and-a-half.

As regards that embarrassing fact, I've taken a very un-random sample of parents of deaf children during the past few years. I find that I was later in discovering Charlie's deafness than some, earlier than others. Of course, discovery is hardly the correct word. Before one can discover something, there has to be inquiry, searching. Before that, one must admit that there is a reason to inquire, something to search for. That is where I dragged my feet. I didn't ask the question because I feared the answer.

There was no lack of indicators of Charlie's hearing loss. His babyhood was replete with clues to his deafness. I know that because I have gone over each of them, incredulous that I missed them the first time through.

Were it not so mortifying, it might be laughable to remember my behavior during those first months with Charlie. Being a foreign-language teacher, I wanted my son to grow up completely bilingual. This I attempted to achieve by talking to Charlie in Spanish during the day, or most of it, and changing to English when his father was home. Of course, Charlie's responses were negligible. In fact, my foreign jabbering probably served to confuse him more. I do not believe that it caused his deafness; more likely my lullaby singing was responsible for that. However, it is possible that the constantly changing speech that Charlie saw overwhelmed him in his neonatal attempts at understanding or imitating speech. That it convinced him he was dealing with a schizophrenic mother, there can be no doubt.

More evidence of my ignorance of Charlie's deafness is shown by my insistence on surrounding him with music. I sang to Charlie (we've discussed that before), and we danced. Behind nearly all our activities was the lilt of a sonata or the thunder of a symphony. I had dreams of my child becoming a classical musician, developing the talent I was sure I had passed on to him. When he would travel on concert tours, I would be with him, enjoying the accolades due the mother of a genius.

I read stories to Charlie, faithfully, so that he could develop the literary skills that he surely had inherited from me. I, of course, held Charlie in my lap during our reading sessions. This meant he could not see my face, so he didn't know I was talking to him. To Charlie, we were simply looking at pictures and turning pages. When we read, Charlie grew impatient after only a few minutes. He insisted on turning the pages, either before or after I finished reading them. Sometimes I became so frustrated that the book would suddenly find itself on the floor across the room. This cathartic action usually produced a giggle from Charlie.

A musical train that had been given to Charlie as an early first-Christmas gift was an object of minimal interest to him.

Even discounting the microscopic attention span of a child between one and two years, I thought it should have produced an occasional squeal of joy, if not silent awe. He had the same reaction to a musical pony attached to his crib. Brahm's Lullaby could be had for a pull on the string. When I pulled the string for him, Charlie watched it ease back into the pony's tummy. He was not, however, motivated to pull it for himself. One morning, awakening at child's dawn, I heard the music. It was the only time he ever produced it to my knowledge. Perhaps a wandering finger or toe merely caught itself in the ring at the end of the string. However the accident came about, Charlie found no reason to try to recreate it.

All of these clues should have alerted me to Charlie's hearing loss. My list of excuses for why they did not is impressive for its length, but the fact refuses to be altered. I did not see Charlie's problem. Suspected? Yes. Ignored? Possibly. Feared? Most definitely.

Even later, when the clues were more evident, I could hardly say that I sought an answer to the question of whether Charlie could hear. More correctly, I inhibited the process.

During the period when I was oblivious to Charlie's hearing loss, my husband and I were having difficulties. One day in the late spring following Charlie's first birthday, my husband announced that he would be bringing his girlfriend to live with him. He suggested that I leave before she arrived. It was the first thing we had agreed on in some time. After six agonizing months as the victim of my husband's indecision over whether he wanted to be married to me or not, I was grateful for this decision even though it went against me.

The only place I could think of for me and Charlie to go was to my parents' home in Kansas City. I needed to find work and a new place to live and a hundred other things that all seemed impossible to do at that point. Mostly, I needed to rest and be with people who cared about me. Charlie needed it, too. For all intents and purposes, Charlie's father disappeared. Charlie saw him only once in the next six years.

I packed whatever I could carry, and Charlie and I left for Kansas City. We looked like refugees. As we disembarked from the plane, I had Charlie on one hip and an overstuffed backpack on the other. In my one relatively free hand, I carried a bundle of diapers wrapped in grocery bags and masking tape. I deposited myself and my son in my parents' house, and we stayed for the next two years. The impact on Charlie was to be immense.

It was immediately evident to my family that Charlie had a hearing problem. He did not answer to his name. ("He is independent. He doesn't want to come over here right now.") He did not speak. ("He is by nature a quiet child. He'll speak when he is ready. Remember, he got his first tooth at thirteen months.") He did not watch television. ("I've never encouraged him to watch. I don't want him to be a tube brat.") One could come up behind Charlie, out of his peripheral vision range, undetected. ("He has very intense concentration. I'm that way myself; you know that.")

I had a reason for all his questionable behavior. I was, after all, the child's mother, and I was responsible for his care. Any deficiencies on his part must have been my responsibility. I hadn't talked to him enough, or maybe I had talked to him too much. Whatever the problem, it would surely remedy itself with maturity. Kids can "outgrow" anything, can't they?

My most convincing excuse was the fact that Charlie had been seen by a legion of doctors for various reasons, and none of them had ever questioned his lack of speech. They usually asked me during the course of an examination if Charlie could hear. That came right along with can he sit up, can he walk, etc., etc. I always said yes. I thought he could hear. Then, as doctors do, they checked for themselves. They clapped their hands. They called his name. One even used a tuning fork. If the doctors were satisfied, who was I to question the academy medicus?

When my family grew tired of listening to my excuses, they initiated the pot-lid banging stage. My parents and other family members recruited to the cause of convincing me that Charlie could not hear, took every occasion to demonstrate Charlie's poor response to loud noises. My father, walking as gingerly as

9

his bulk allowed, would come up behind Charlie clapping his hands. My mother, armed with pot lid and wooden spoon, would tiptoe up to Charlie's back while another conspirator diverted his attention. Then, the clang of wood on metal. No response, of course. "Now, you can't possibly ignore something like that," one of them would say.

"Are you telling me how to raise my own son?" I'd ask defensively.

There it was. That most dreaded of all maternal plagues—grandparental interference. I now had a new defense and a new diversion from Charlie's problem. But, since I obviously needed the support and help of my family in reestablishing my single life, I settled upon a compromise. I would ask a doctor, albeit a pediatrician, for an assessment of Charlie's problem. Charlie was due for a checkup, and we needed to establish ourselves with a new doctor, so all would be satisfied.

The appointment time came; I can still feel the grinding of my teeth as my mother said, "Be sure to ask the doctor about testing Charlie's hearing. Do you want me to go with you?"

"No."

"Who'll know if I ask him," I thought in the waiting room. Charlie was staring at the other kids in the waiting room, as was his custom, but not joining in. "He's a loner, like his mother," I assured myself.

Our names were called and we went into an examination room for the second round of waiting. At last the doctor appeared. I asked and answered the rapid-fire questions of a busy pediatrician until I realized that the examination was over and the doctor was halfway out the door.

"By the way, can you test his hearing?"

The doctor turned around to face me, the lower part of his body continuing on its way out the door. I was clearly breaking his sprint to the next patient. "Oh, let's wait until he is two." (Aha! You see, he hadn't noticed any problem.) It was not obvious to the doctor in the two to three minutes spent with my child that he couldn't hear. Besides, waiting until Charlie turned two was sound medical practice. It takes a couple of years for the kinks in children to work themselves out. Anyone should know you can't really tell much of anything about a child until the child is two.

I had been given a reprieve. Medical proof positive that my family was wrong. They were wrong to question Charlie and wrong to question me. I'm a good mother; my son couldn't be deaf. In the car, on the way home, I told Charlie, "Now, we have exactly six months in which you must learn to talk. That's not much time, but I think we can do it. We'll forget about the Spanish for now. No more attempts at bilingualism. Obviously, that is what has confused you. We'll both work very hard and you'll be talking like crazy by two." Charlie didn't respond. The rhythm of the car had put him to sleep, I explained to myself.

The days passed quickly. I used every minute out of my family's view to work on Charlie's speech. I set him on my lap, with or without cooperation, with a book, magazine, or pad of paper. I named objects; I repeated and recited words, phrases, and stories. I drew pictures, pointed to them, and named them. Charlie would point at the picture without making any sound. ("That will come. Give him time. He has six months, remember.") When I felt confident that I had drilled him enough, I said the word without pointing to the picture. Occasionally, as the law of averages would dictate, Charlie made a correct choice. ("See there family!") More often, the responses were inaccurate. I moved his finger to the correct picture, reinforcing by repeating the proper word. Charlie grabbed my finger and pounded it all over the page. I slapped his hand. The game was over. I made a few more attempts to force his finger to the right spot, until a combination of Charlie's squirming and my guilt at failure gave him his freedom from my lap.

I was losing valuable time. As my confidence in being able to teach Charlie to talk turned first to frustration and then to panic, I saw a calendar on every face. I knew what the family was thinking—"Only five more months to make him talk. Even a good mother couldn't do that."

11

Then, just as I was becoming convinced of a family conspiracy to prove me unfit, I hit upon a new explanation. "Any child put through the kinds of life disruptions Charlie has recently experienced might withdraw, be reluctant to talk. Can't all of you see that?" I asked the family. "This child has been uprooted, has left the only home he ever knew. How bewildered he must be. One day he has a mommy and daddy, and the next day only a mommy. Now he has a mommy and two grandparents. The familiar surroundings of his infancy have been snatched from him. The blue rug, the blonde crib with peeling Bambi decals, the paint-spattered hardwood floors. This was the only world he knew, and it has suddenly been replaced by a suburban ranch and kitchen carpet. Then, as though all that upheaval weren't enough, his mother goes off to work, leaving him all day with an aunt he barely knows. 'Why is Mommy leaving me here?' he must wonder. You have to realize, Charlie is trying to put his shattered world back together again. He has no time to talk." I convinced no one in the family; I barely convinced myself.

2

I began job hunting soon after we had settled into my parents' home. Finding a job wasn't difficult. At least I knew what to expect; I had worked up until Charlie was born. Someone once told me that a woman who can type will never starve. Even for a woman with a college degree that maxim holds true. So, I became a secretary. This was just temporary I told myself. I quickly added underemployed to my list of Reasons Why I Justifiably Feel Sorry for Myself.

While I was busy being (and making those around me) miserable, my family persisted in their support. Charlie developed a closeness to my father that transcended communication. My brother's wife, Betty, kept Charlie while I worked. She became his second mother, and she was able to elicit behavior from Charlie I had thought I would have to wait years to see. My brother and sister offered their attention, their caring, and their money, by turns, in support. I'm sure that it must have been difficult at times to put up with my pessimism, but no one ever lost patience with what I was going through. Jealous of their closeness to and success with Charlie, I repeatedly bit the hands they offered. Whether their faith was in Charlie or in me, I hope I never find out. They pulled me through. I kicked all the way.

My mother fell victim to the worst abuse. In that natural competition between mother and grown daughter, I was a tough opponent. My mother, whose traditional unassertiveness could make me furious, turned out to be the strong one. I was the one whose marriage had failed. I was the one with the imperfect child. I was the one running away from problems, both Charlie's and mine. For all my education and my self-sufficiency, I was the one who had run to her for help. She gave it in abundance. Unappreciated and even resented, she kept on giving. I think that while everyone else saw Charlie's problems as paramount, Mom knew the real problem was me.

One Saturday afternoon, Mom and I were the only ones home with Charlie. We had planned an afternoon shopping trip. We were trying to feed Charlie lunch so that we could go and get back before his nap time. Charlie was hungry, but for what? It was the same game we played every day.

"What do you want, Charlie?" No response.

I stood at the refrigerator, taking out one item after another. "Do you want cheese?" No response. Not a nod, not a smile, not a line changed on his face. "Do you want a hot dog?" Still nothing.

"Maybe he wants some cereal," Mom suggested.

"He had that for breakfast. But, if he doesn't care, I don't." I held up the oatmeal box. Charlie's expression changed slightly. "You want cereal?" I asked, nodding. Charlie moved his head in rhythm with mine. Good enough for me.

"Do you want me to fix it for him," Mom offered.

"I think I can handle instant oatmeal," I snapped.

"I thought you might need to get ready to go, or something."

"No, thanks. If he doesn't get moving, no one is going anywhere."

Mom kept Charlie occupied while I made cereal. When I was convinced it had cooled enough for him, without actually tasting the stuff, I set the bowl down in front of Charlie. He looked at it and at me, surprised. Then, he pushed the bowl away.

"Charlie, you said you wanted cereal."

"Come on, Charlie," Mom said, pulling the bowl toward her. "Grandma will help you." But, he didn't even eat it for her.

"Okay," I snorted. "One more try and that's it." I pulled out the peanut butter and held it up for Charlie to see. "Do you want this?" His smile and reaching hand seemed a stronger yes vote than for the cereal. "Okay. Then, it's peanut butter. I'll save your oatmeal for dinner. Should be really yukky by then."

I delivered the peanut butter sandwich to Charlie. He didn't push it away but kept pointing toward the kitchen.

"Now what?" I screamed right in his face. My mother was already holding the sandwich up for him to take a bite. "Let him hold it for himself." I was screaming at her now. Charlie began to cry while he continued to point.

"Maybe he wants some milk," Mom offered.

"Then let him ask for it. What do you want, Charlie? You little retard." I left the room shaking. I sat on the basement steps and sobbed. In the kitchen, I heard my mother's voice break as she said, "Here's some milk, Charlie. Let's make the sandwich all gone."

I felt hideous. I trembled with frustration. I had turned a simple lunch into a nightmare. My mother came up behind me and quietly said in a clear voice, "Don't call him retarded."

This was the worst episode I can remember, but the frustration of communicating with Charlie grew each day. He couldn't talk. He couldn't even nod coherently. I'd get mad, then he'd get mad. Something was wrong, I knew. "God," I prayed, "let us make it through, somehow, until he's two."

Not long after that lunch, I arrived home from work one afternoon and Mom handed me a note.

"Who called?" I asked, in the conversation-discouraging tone I had adopted in those days.

"It's not a message," she said, turning away. My mother's style is to lessen the impact of bad news by giving it from hiding. Not poor judgment considering my mood those days. "I called Dr. Whitaker. You remember him. He took out Mike's and Marlena's tonsils. He's an ear, nose, and throat specialist."

"I know who he is."

She turned full face toward me. I set my feet. "You may hate me for this for the rest of my life. I can't help that, but if you won't take him, I will."

("You wouldn't drive that far," I thought.) "And?" I asked aloud.

"I talked to his audiologist." Every muscle in my body tensed. "She said that Charlie is not too young to have his hearing tested. She said it is important to test him early. There are funds available from the state to help pay for it, and if they won't, I will."

"Okay, I'll call her."

"When?"

"Well, I doubt that she's there now. I'll call her tomorrow, if I get a chance."

"I'll call her tomorrow." Mom's voice had an unfamiliar note of finality.

"I said I would call and I will."

She turned away again. "It might be correctable, you know."

Correctable. Of course. A minor obstruction. A faulty mechanism. Something out of place, out of tune. Snip, snip, stitch, stitch, and we're back in business. "I'll call her tomorrow and make an appointment." But, my mother had left the room already. A tidal wave of guilt rolled over me for the way I had talked to her. I did nothing except roll with it.

I did not call the next morning. It was a busy day at work, although no more so than any other. By late afternoon, however, I realized I was facing the prospect of "Did you call today?" when I returned home, so I called.

"Oh yes, I talked to your mother yesterday, wasn't it? It sounds like your little boy may have a hearing problem." I wondered how much my mother had revealed about me as well as about Charlie.

"How reliable are hearing tests on someone his age?" (Please say, "Not very.")

"Quite reliable. How old is . . . what's his name?"

"Charlie."

"Cute name. We test children under one year with very good results." (I was already six months late.) "Of course, the testing

16

process is an ongoing one in young children. We test periodically as they grow to more closely define the extent and type of loss they may have. But, we can tell quite accurately how much of a loss he has, even at his age."

We went through some further encouraging chitchat while the audiologist looked up the name of someone to contact at the state-run Crippled Children's Service. "She can help you with the testing and so on. Go ahead and give her a call, but in the meantime, we can test Charlie right away for you. I'll transfer you to the receptionist for an appointment. Do you have any more questions?"

"What kind of . . . how often is a problem such as this correctable?"

"Well, let's talk about that when you bring Charlie in, okay?"

"Sure."

"Hold on now, I'll get the receptionist for you."

So, the appointment was made. I had this feeling of irreversibility that made me nauseous. "Now you have done it," I told myself. "You have announced to the world that your son can't hear. Now, for the coup de grace, call the state and ask them to pay for it." Had I been less irrational, I probably could have come up with a reason why all of this was Charlie's father's fault. Charlie was withdrawn because of our separation, or something equally absurd. No, it was all clearly my fault, somehow. The hearing problem, the state, all of it. My fault.

The logistics of getting Charlie and me to the appointment with the audiologist rivaled the Normandy invasion in its complexity. My mother wanted to go but feared asking. I clearly could not go alone without making a trip back home to deliver Charlie to his Aunt Betty's house before going on to work. For Betty to go meant her son Marc must also go. My father offered to go, but I was beginning to feel a bit like a tour director, so I bluntly refused.

For my part, I wanted only the essential parties to this mission. Ever one to selfishly horde my misery, I resented my sister-in-law's having to accompany us, even though I was forced to give in to it. It was necessary. I was taught early on that missing work falls within the category of sins such as sloth, greed, and lack of discipline. Betty would bring Charlie back while I went on to work. Somehow, I felt that my going to work lent an aura of normality to the proceedings. If we could keep a few things within the scope of reality, perhaps the rest would follow along.

The caravan departed on schedule. Two cars were needed. Charlie was fascinated with this arrangement. He watched out the back window to see Aunt Betty and Marc waving dutifully from their car. For him, this was a lark, equal to all the delights his days held.

We all arrived. We even parked next to each other, if memory serves. We resembled a family outing or a stroll into an amusement park. Marc and Charlie scampered ahead. For them, this day held some of life's joys: a ride in the car and in an elevator, perhaps the prospect of some treat from the drugstore in the building's lobby. I tried to remain open-minded and optimistic. This was not from knowing that the outcome of this visit, whatever it might be, could be dealt with, handled, overcome. My lack of feeling was from the sincere belief that if I didn't want it to, this would not turn out badly.

The doctor's waiting room was impressive for its size, its neatness, and its pile of toys stacked in the corner.

"We must be the first kids of the day," I told Betty, motioning to the toys waiting neatly for the chaos about to be perpetrated by our boys. She smiled. I made a mental note that wit implies bravery and resolved to be at my keenest for the doctor.

Betty supervised the boys while I took care of all the financial questions at the receptionist's desk. When I mentioned that I did not have any medical insurance as yet, having just started a job, the receptionist gave me a muffled groan. I explained that I was going through the Crippled Children's Service, and she said, "Oh," in a knowing tone. She marked my file accordingly. I felt the red acronym signifying the state was as indelible on my forehead as on the file folder. It would now appear in all my son's records and would follow him through his life. Everywhere he went—to school, for a job, before the Nobel Prize selection committee—that acronym would follow him. A *state* child.

In reconstructing my feeling about that day, I always imagine myself falling down a flight of stairs. Not all at once, but falling down one stair at a time. After a few moments of comfort, thinking I've surely reached the bottom, I fall to the next step. Each time the same hard bump, the same loud thump.

I was just pulling myself up from the first fall when the audiologist came out to greet us. She was tall, athletic, and slender, with a warm smile. Prepared to dispute everything I would hear on this visit, I distrusted her immediately. She couldn't possibly be a competent professional. She had the look of a woman who went out at night; she probably water skied or ran marathons on her lunch hour. She should have gone straight home to read and reread the instructions on how to test the hearing of small boys. She should not have been so confident when she was obviously about to make a big mistake.

"Hi, I'm Alice. Hello, Charlie." No response. I noticed the elevated volume and special attention to enunciation in her speech. She was already talking to Charlie as if he were deaf. I resented her assumption. "He's too busy to pay attention," I explained nervously. The first words out of my mouth had made me sound like an idiot. Her confidence contrasted with my incompetence to make it seem gargantuan. We followed Alice back to the examination rooms. The short and unsure following the tall and confident. She was determined to contrast with me.

The doctor's office was arranged in a labyrinth. The corridors from the waiting room turned to the right and then to the left, like a set of eustachian tubes. Here were the examining rooms, the audiology booth, and a second nurse's station. An EXIT sign marked the only way out. One way traffic around and through. I was not surprised to find the cashier's office around the corner; it was the last stop before finding oneself deposited in the hall. A bit surrealistic for my taste, but obviously a successful arrangement.

Charlie and I followed Alice past an examining room with a table. Poised above the table, looking like an X-ray machine, was what I later learned was a huge microscope. The patient lying on the table looked up at a blue sky complete with five-pointed stars, a smiling moon, and a rainbow in the corner. I felt a twinge of sympathy for the state at having to support this kind of overhead.

Our examining room lay beyond. It was directly across from the audiology booth. Alice led us into the examining room and placed our folder in the slot outside. I noticed that the red state marker was clearly displayed.

Charlie had enjoyed the walk. With so much to see, he ambled slowly, turning his head from side to side. He looked so tiny, still a baby. What was he doing here. He looked at everything with wide eyes. His little mouth gaped open slightly in concentration between the twin domes of his baby cheeks. Why had I brought an infant to a place like this?

As Alice moved farther ahead of us, I picked Charlie up so as not to lose her or give the impression of not being able to keep up. When we arrived in our appointed room, he squirmed his way out of my arms and began to climb into the big examining chair. Once there, he climbed immediately down and began pulling tissues out of the box on a small writing table. I was holding a rather large handful of these tissues, preparing to dispose of them, when a well-scrubbed doctor put his head in the door and smiled. ("A welfare patient stealing Kleenex," I perceived him to be thinking.) "Why don't you step across the hall, and let Alice test Charlie. I'll see you when she is finished. Alice is very good, and I rely on her findings." I turned to pick Charlie up and said, "Come on, Charlie. Let's go see Alice, now." I thought if the doctor heard me talking to Charlie he would realize that he couldn't be deaf. When I turned back, the doctor was gone. Taking my opportunity to dispose of the tissues, I did so and grabbed Charlie before he could do further damage. We crossed the Rubicon hall.

Once in the room containing the audiology booth, the vault-like door caught my attention. It seemed unchallengeable, just as its findings would be. Charlie was fascinated and delighted with the new sights—buttons and lights and little toys. We went into the booth where Charlie found some little blocks and expropriated them.

"Do you think he'll sit in here by himself?" Alice asked.

"I doubt it."

"Okay. You sit in the chair and just let him sit on your lap."

Alice spent several minutes trying to show Charlie what was expected of him. He was to drop a plastic block into a coffee can if he heard something. Alice pointed to her ear and smiled an exaggerated smile, her eyes wide. Then she dropped a block in the can. I thought this process a bit complex for someone only eighteen months old and decided the test couldn't be valid.

We positioned ourselves in the booth, facing a window behind which Alice would sit at her control panel. On either side of the booth stood large stage amplifiers. To the left was a small table holding more equipment. Alice put headphones on me similar to those worn by people working on airport runways. She cautioned me not to signal Charlie in any way. Then, she shut and, I thought, locked the booth door. Charlie held tight to his blocks and made a grab for my earphones. I turned him around and pointed to Alice. She began.

She called to Charlie first on one amplifier and then the other, while holding a piece of paper over her mouth. He did not turn. She turned up the volume, and I sat as rigid as possible so as not to give anything away. I could, however, feel the muscles in my legs flexing on either the right or the left, depending on where the sound was. Involuntary help, but of no help at all. Charlie dropped all the blocks in his hand into the coffee can at one time.

Next came sounds of different frequency and loudness, first on the left and then on the right. Two lefts and then a right; the pattern was completely random. Once or twice there was an indecisive turn of the head from Charlie. The dropping of the blocks continued in a meaningless pattern. I could feel myself being pitched down several stairs at once.

Mercifully, Charlie soon tired of this. When I was sure that we had lost him to the blocks, I slipped one of my ear coverings off. The sound literally knocked me back in the chair.

Alice tried some other tests using earphones to test his resistance to the pressure of sound. She continually complimented me on Charlie's amazing cooperation. I was somewhat less happy with the cooperation due to the results we were getting, or that I thought we might be getting. I still held hope that I was reading the signs wrong and that she would say everything was fine at the end of the ordeal.

When we were freed from the booth, Alice made some notes. Charlie was busy looking around at everything in the room, and I was busy trying to keep from coming apart. The graph Alice was constructing was meaningless to me. I could tell, though, that all the marks were at the bottom of the page, and that didn't seem good.

After a time, Alice laid down her pencil and gave me her full attention. Her hands were folded professionally in her lap. "Of course, this is only a very superficial test, and we will need to continue to test Charlie, but, it appears that he has no usable hearing."

My eyes filled. Alice talked some more about testing and therapy and some other things that I missed. I perceived from her tone that she was trying to be optimistic and comforting. She put her hand on my arm. I felt small and ugly, as though I had become hideous and disgusting and worthy of pity. My lips curled in nausea. I looked at Charlie. He was still holding his blocks and looking about the room with his most beguiling wide-eyed expression. I think Alice commented on how beautiful and sweet he was. Through quivering lips, I asked, "Can he learn to talk?"

"Of course. It will take time. It won't be easy. But, I went to school with a deaf girl who had just beautiful speech. You could hardly tell. Charlie's a bright little boy. He'll learn to talk." I think that was what she said.

Then, we were back across the hall. Things were happening very fast now. As I tell them, they seem so logical and correct.

But then, the people and the words were streaking past me. I wanted the doctor to think I was competent, so I tried to think of questions to ask that made sense. I avoided the only real question I had, "Why?"

Dr. Whitaker gave Charlie what struck me as a standard pediatric examination. And then, he asked the questions. They brought me temporarily back. I had to help the doctor with all the information I could think of, which would help him explain why this had happened and what could be done about it. We discussed Charlie's birth. Difficult. We went through all the details.

"And Charlie's father?"

"We're separated."

"I see. Any history of hearing problems in either his or your families?"

"No, none that I know about."

We talked more, Charlie went along easily with it all. Dr. Whitaker offered no indication that any of the medical history I was giving him was significant to Charlie's deafness. Then, he said, "I'm going to have Alice come in and fit Charlie for his body aid. We might as well get as much done as we can while he's still cooperating. He's a very good boy."

"A body aid?" (Now we're talking about his whole body?)

"It's the type of hearing aid worn on the chest. You've probably seen them. They are the older type, but they are really the best for sound reception. We start children with them. When children get older, we fit them with hearing aids that hook behind the ear."

"How much will a hearing aid help?"

"You'll be surprised at the difference it makes. Of course, with a loss such as Charlie's, it won't give him normal hearing. It will enhance the hearing he does have and help him pick up vibrations."

"Then he can hear some?"

"Oh yes. No one is totally without sound. But, he can't hear speech. The aid will help him with environmental sounds. He'll

23

do very well with it, I'm sure. It won't be easy. You have a long road ahead. You'll have to get him into special day care, speech therapy, and special education as soon as possible, but he'll be just fine."

By this time, Charlie had squirmed out of the chair and was opening the door. My mind was back on all the special help that I was responsible for giving Charlie. Where would I find it? How would I get him there? How would I pay for all of this? Charlie was now opening the door.

"We'd better get Alice in here before we lose him," the doctor said. I forced a smile.

The doctor left and Charlie went right behind him. I let him go for a minute so I could collect myself. When responsibility overtook me, I went to fetch Charlie. I found him flirting with the woman in the next examining room. "Hello, little boy. What's your name?" She talked to him as though she couldn't see that he couldn't hear her. Maybe she couldn't. Half an hour before, I had been just like her—ignorant but content.

Alice and I retrieved Charlie and brought him back to our room. The next part was great fun for him. Alice mixed a powder and water into a pasty putty and kneaded it in her hands. She peeled off a small piece and gave it to Charlie to play with. I was proud of him. He was still the same little boy I brought in, and yet, he would never be the same for me.

"Should I still talk to him?"

Alice was kind—or perceptive—enough not to look at me incredulously. She must have heard other equally stupid questions before.

"Oh, of course, You don't want to treat him differently than you would a hearing child. Just make sure he's looking at you when you talk to him. That is how he will learn to read lips."

"I used to teach Spanish," I told her for some reason.

"Then you know about teaching language. That gives you a big head start." She was much more confident of that than I was.

Charlie held very still while Alice stuffed the hardening pink putty into his ears. "Most kids scream at this," she said. After a

24

few minutes of tickling and playing with Charlie while the molds congealed, she removed them.

"Now, I'll send these off to get his first set of ear molds made for his hearing aid. It should be ready in about two weeks. We'll call you and you can bring Charlie in to have it fitted. We'll probably test him again then. Okay, Charlie?" She left saying that the doctor wanted to talk with me some more.

Then, she was gone. I was alone with a restless boy who couldn't hear me. I picked him up and held him tight. We walked over to the window that overlooked the parking lot, and I held the curtain back for Charlie to see. I pointed to the cars and told him the colors and counted them for him. We saw a bird light on the grass and peck around before flying away, free. We saw people coming in and going out of the building. I kept up a steady chatter in an effort to keep from having to think about what was happening.

Something began to take shape in the back of my mind; as it moved closer to the front it became clearer, until finally, it dominated my mind's eye like a movie screen. Music. My son would never hear music. Then, it all fell apart; my composure, my determination to have them all believe I could handle it. I sobbed on Charlie's little shoulder, racking, silent sobs. He became very still. He had seen me cry before, and it always made him respectfully quiet. No music. How could there be life without music? My mind was spinning. Hearing aids, therapy, special schools. Where? How? Who?

Dr. Whitaker returned. We stayed at the window a minute, then sat in one of the extra chairs lined against the wall opposite the examining chair. He sat next to me, a gesture I felt was indicative of the gravity of the situation. We weren't sitting below him now, as we had in the examining chair. He held a small cross-section model of an ear. I heard very little of his explanation.

"Is there anything you want to ask?"

"I don't know right now. I need to think."

"Sure. Call me or Alice, any time. She can probably put you in touch with some teachers or parents to talk to, if you like.

"Okay."

He put his hand on my arm. "Charlie will be all right," he said. Even in my confusion, I was aware of his concern. We sat quietly for a minute. Charlie, from sensing the atmosphere or just being tired, had become quiet, too. The doctor rose to leave. His hand was on the door knob when I whispered, "Can it be corrected?" Turning, I saw his face and knew the answer.

"No. I wish it could be. Charlie's ear structures are fine. There is no obstruction. Maybe some day, but not now. I'm sorry." He wanted to leave and I let him go.

"Let's go, baby," I said to my deaf son.

We left the examining room and completed the maze of corridors to find ourselves deposited in the hall. It impressed me as being the loser's shoot of a cheap quiz show. I had to go back into the reception area to pick up Betty and Marc, who were waiting in roughly the same condition as when we went in. There was no great mystery as to the outcome of the examination. My red face and puffy eyes told the whole story. Charlie ran back to the toys. Betty and I stood amid the clutter of toys and magazines and held each other. I don't remember saying anything, and there was certainly no need.

"Why don't you come back home with us? Call work and tell them you won't be in," she suggested. It was appealing. The thought of meeting the concerned but questioning faces of my co-workers was frightening. They knew where I had gone and why. I was not really prepared to make explanations about something I could not begin to understand.

But, what would I do with myself at home? For one thing, I would have to think about this new situation. When I looked at Charlie, I saw a stranger. He would never again be the child he was, or at least the child I had seen him to be. I would have to redefine him. It seemed as though I would have to reacquaint myself with him. At work, my thoughts could be otherwise occupied. A short-term escape, surely, but going to work, even with all its questions, seemed the better choice. There was plenty of time to deal with Charlie later. There would be a lifetime for that.

We left the doctor's office, walked silently to the cars, and separated. Watching Charlie I began to resent his sameness, his happiness. He acted as if nothing had changed. Climbing into Betty's car to share a back seat ride with Marc did not seem different to him. His world had not changed, while mine had collapsed. I turned and got into my car.

The office where I worked was a short distance from the doctor's office. Too short for me to prepare myself to meet people. What would I say? My eyes were filling up again, and I blinked wildly to see. The task of rehearsing my words to my friends kept me together. "Charlie can't hear as well as he should. Charlie has a hearing loss. Charlie is hearing impaired." I knew all the euphemisms to protect me from the word *deaf*.

Arriving at work, I sat in the parking lot trying to repair my face in the rearview mirror. I am one of those unfortunates cursed with skin that reddens and blotches when I cry for prolonged periods. My mirror revealed eyes that were slits between puffed lids, a red nose, swollen lips, and blotchy cheeks. Nothing was hidden. My attempts at camouflage a failure, I headed for the bathroom to try cold paper towels. Equally ineffective. Finally, there remained only to go through the halls to my office. Back stiff, head up, red faced, I walked past everyone. I think they looked up at me, but they probably missed the effect of a full front view.

I sat in the office I shared with a colleague for a few minutes before my friends began coming in. One by one, they asked the same question, "What did you find out?"

"Well, Charlie does have a hearing problem, but with a hearing aid and special school, he'll do fine." After several repetitions it became easier to say, almost believable.

It was time to call my mother. She had been waiting all this time for a call I had promised to make as soon as we were finished at the doctor's office. I went over the call in my mind— "You were right, Mom. You were all right. He's deaf as a post. Bye, now. See you at dinner." She had made me take him to the doctor. We could all have been happy in our ignorance, for a bit longer at least. After all, as long as I didn't know Charlie couldn't

27

hear, there was a chance that he could. My thinking was garbled, confused, and irrational, but I did know that I couldn't blame my mother. It was at that moment that I laid the blame where I thought it clearly belonged, on me. (It was to remain there for some time.) Then, I picked up the phone.

"Hi, Mom."

"Hello."

"Well, Charlie does have a loss. It's pretty bad. The phrase Alice used was *no usable hearing*. But, we're getting him a hearing aid and that should be a big help."

"I'm so sorry."

"Me, too. What a bunch of shit."

"What do we do now? I mean, are they sure?"

"I guess so. We aren't scheduled to go back. That's it."

"We'll work it out somehow. Charlie's bright and we'll all help. Did you ask about it being correctable, you know, by an operation or something?"

"Yes, Mother," my voice icy. "I asked all the right questions. It can't be fixed. That's it. He can't hear and that's it. (Damn it. Why can't I stop myself from attacking her?) I have to get some work done. See you later."

"Hello, Alice? This is Mar . . . Charlie's mother."

"Oh yes, how are you?"

"All right."

"Charlie's hearing aid order has gone in, and we should be getting it in two or three weeks."

"That's fine. What I'm calling about is . . . Do you think that the other day when we were in . . . that perhaps there might have been a problem with the equipment? I mean, could there be some mistake about Charlie? He is pretty good at ignoring people when he wants to. I think he might have simply not understood what he was supposed to do."

Silence.

"I'd like to have him tested again."

28

"Well, I'll certainly be glad to do the test again, but I really don't think the results will be any different this time. We've been testing other people with the same equipment and it's working fine."

"I know, but Charlie is so young, and everything was new and confusing to him. I'm sure he would do better this time."

"Have you been in touch with the people from the state agency?"

"Yes. Well, I have an appointment to talk with one of their people."

"That's good. I really doubt that they would pay for a second test so soon, but if you want to make an appointment, I'll be glad to retest Charlie. Why don't you think about it a little while?"

"All right. It's just that . . ."

"I know how difficult this must be for you. Tell you what. Why don't you try some things at home with Charlie to see if you can get him to respond. If you do, then you call me and we'll talk some more about retesting Charlie, okay?"

"Thank you," I said as I put down the phone. But what I thought was, "No thank you! No more pot-lid banging. No more sneaking up and shouting. No more tapping under the table. I can't go through watching him hungrily for some response. I can't go through seeing that blank look on his face."

Any freshman psychology student can tell you the stages of dealing with tragedy. Disbelief, mourning, anger, grasping at false hope, and resignation, or something along those lines. My disbelief was short lived. Mourning manifested itself in not speaking to Charlie, or to anyone else. I unplugged my radio and refused to watch television. I surrounded myself with the absence of sound so as to make sound not exist. It was impossible to live with the fact that Charlie could not experience sound.

I might have passed over the grasping-at-false-hope stage, if not encouraged by others. My sense of hopelessness would not allow me to seek other doctors, much less healers, experiments, or miracle devices. I did learn through well-meaning others of

29

everything from deaf people being cured by lightning to experiments with surgical implants in the ear. Every so often I received in the mail an article cut from a supermarket magazine—Diet Cures Deafness, Acupuncture Works, Hypnosis Halts Hearing Loss, even Bizarre Objects Found Lodged in Ears of People Thought Deaf for Years. I was not ungrateful, but I never read the clippings. I had to believe that Charlie was deaf, forever. This had to be the end of the disappointments. If I accepted this last defeat, perhaps the stone-hearted Fates would let up on us.

Of the five stages of coping with tragedy, the one I found most difficult to escape was anger. Anger at a creator who, in an instant of carelessness or inattention, allowed this to happen. Anger at the scientific community for not having at their fingertips some remedy for Charlie. Anger at the whole world for its misplaced emphasis on sound and speech and music. Anger at myself for being so helpless.

I often wonder what Charlie must have thought about those first few weeks of deafness. Of course, nothing had changed for him except his mother's behavior. Mama didn't talk to him anymore. Mama stayed in her room most of the time. Mama cried a lot. I could not understand his sameness. He should have been drastically different. He was deaf. Some new grotesqueness should have showed up on him somewhere. But it didn't. All my dreams and plans for him had been snuffed out in one short morning. There would be no music lessons, no long talks. How could he be happy when so much of what I enjoyed was lost to him? Yet, it was just this happiness, this sameness, that finally brought me out of my melancholy and around to doing some real good for Charlie. If baby Charlie could handle this, then so would I.

It was nearly two weeks to the day when Charlie's body aid came in. Alice called me and said she would come in on Saturday to fit Charlie so I wouldn't have to miss work. I was finding so many helpful, generous people around me these days that it was almost an effort to be miserable. Still, I did manage to put forth the effort most of the time.

On the appointed Saturday, we went back to the doctor's office. It was our first time back since the diagnosis of Charlie's deafness. I had not demanded a retest after all, more because I didn't want to hear the bad news again than from any expectation of good. I was determined to put forth the effort necessary to appear that we were coping.

The reception room was full that day. Charlie headed directly for the toys in the waiting room while I announced our arrival. When I joined Charlie at the toy corner, I had this ridiculous urge to call for everyone's attention.

> *Ladies and gentlemen, if I could have your attention for just a moment. This is my son, and he is deaf. No usable hearing at all. I'm not ignoring him, you see. It's simply that he can't hear. Thank you. Please just go back to waiting and staring at us.*

This was the first time I had been aware of Charlie's being watched. More specifically, of his being watched for being different rather than for being gorgeous. I wondered if the people watching us two weeks ago had thought he was different, or if I was giving signals that alerted them now. No, Charlie was so beautiful they must have noticed him first.

Alice had a little box waiting for us in her office. It looked like a jeweler's box for a watch or a bracelet. She opened the box to reveal the body aid. It was slightly smaller than a pack of cigarettes, and it had wires coming out of either side. Next, she brought out a little white harness-like garment. As I watched her put it on Charlie, it reminded me of a one-cup bra, and I said so. Obviously an old line with audiologists. Alice explained about the care of the aid and of the ear molds as she plugged everything together. She put first one ear mold and then the other into Charlie's ears. He stood most cooperatively all the while. When it was finally on, I felt my lip curl. How big it was, covering nearly the whole center of his less than two-year-old chest. The white straps of the carrier contrasted with his dark T-shirt and seemed flourescent in their brightness.

The ear molds were more obvious than I had expected. Little buttons (the receivers) were attached to the ear molds. From these hung what seemed like several feet of wire tightly curled from having been coiled since their manufacture. Charlie looked deaf. For the first time in all of this, Charlie's handicap was obvious to anyone, even without their trying to talk to him. I felt sick. I could not wrench from my mind the memory of a picture I had once seen in a history book of a blind man begging during the Depression. He wore a placard around his neck which read "BLIND." My son now wore the indisputable proof of his abnormality. His sign read "DEAF," and it was just as repugnant to me as the blind man's label.

Alice tried to test Charlie's hearing with the aid on, but the newness of the contraption distracted him from the test. "You can bring him back when he gets used to wearing it. After I test him, we can make some adjustments in the aid so it will do him the most good."

"How much do you think he will be able to hear, now?"

"It's hard to say. It could give him 20 or 30 decibels." I looked confused, so Alice showed me his audiogram. "See, unaided Charlie is here [the bottom of the chart]. A good aid could bring him up maybe to here." She moved her finger slightly up the vertical line of the graph.

"Where is normal hearing?" I asked.

"Here," she said, indicating with her other hand a point nearly at the top of the chart. "Normal hearing goes down to between 10 to 15 decibels." Alice knew I was looking at the universe between her two fingers. "It's a help," she said, almost scolding. "Not enough," I thought.

When Alice turned Charlie's aid on for the first time, I watched his face for a miracle. "Wow, that's much better," I hoped he would say. "Thanks, Mom." There was no detectable reaction.

Charlie was by now becoming restless and cranky. It was almost his nap time, and he was clearly bored with my lingering to chat. Perhaps he also felt left out even though he was the center of our attention. I was beginning to sense that Charlie's deafness would take over our lives from now on and that we would become more closely tied than we were already. Add now to the roles of mother, cook, nurse, chauffeur, valet, etc., etc., teacher and interpreter.

Alice saw that Charlie wanted to go, so she hastily added, "A hearing aid is like glasses or contact lenses. People have to get accustomed to wearing them. Leave the aid on for a while; when he gets tired of it, take it off. Then, increase the time he wears it until he wears it all the time he is awake. Okay? You can start introducing Charlie to different sounds to see how much he is getting."

Alice gave me a booklet on hearing aid care and walked us through the labyrinth to the hall. "Don't be surprised if Charlie acts a little strangely. The new sounds and vibrations he may be getting could be confusing to him for a while."

Grateful that we did not have to face the gawkers in the waiting room with Charlie thus wired for sound, we left by the back way. I was determined to help Charlie discover new sounds and to be considerate of his confusion or discomfort. So far, Charlie had made no attempt to pull the ear molds out, nor had he tried to play with the aid. He wore it indifferently. In the car, going home, he fell asleep with it on, and he wore it effortlessly until bedtime.

When we arrived home, the family stood by the garage door trying to look as if it were usual to stand there. They examined Charlie's new hardware as casually as they could. Charlie seemed not to understand what caused all the attention, but he didn't mind it. As soon as I was able to get all the way into the house, I removed the aid and its carrier and put the whole thing back on him, this time underneath his shirt. Now, only the wires coming out from his collar and the lump in the middle of his chest gave it away. It remained concealed whenever possible until he started school. I then learned that it should be worn outside his clothes because the rubbing of the fabric over the aid caused static. Another in a long line of mistakes made to appease my vanity.

I was enthusiastic about introducing Charlie to sound. The whole world was waiting for him, and I was going to help him discover it, immediately. First, we tried the old standards. Pot-lid banging came back into vogue. Charlie did not seem to hear it any better than before. No matter, there were plenty more sounds to try. I was, of course, eager to get him started on music. This I did by showing him the stereo. I'd put on a record, turn up the volume, and watch his face. Nothing. I'd try to hold his hand on the speaker thinking that feeling the vibrations would help him concentrate. "Do you hear it?" I'd ask, my face bursting with enthusiastic hopefulness. I'd point to my ear. He'd point to his ear and smile, too. Then, I'd turn the music off and say, "I don't hear it," pointing to my ear as I shook my head in a sad no. Charlie would point to his ear and smile.

Proud at first of Charlie's maturity and tolerance in wearing the hearing aid without a fuss, I soon began to wonder if he was getting any new sounds with it. His reaction to it was as if it weren't there at all. Was this good? Did the aid do him any good? I confess that I still wonder that today. Charlie is the only one who can judge the aid's effectiveness and within the next few years he will decide if it makes communicaton easier or simply amplifies the garbled mess his auditory nerves send to his brain. It is despicable to admit that I hope he rejects it, even the behind-the-ear aid he now wears. I have still not overcome the sign, "DEAF," that the aid flashes to the world. Perhaps I am somewhat redeemed for insisting that Charlie wear his aid as much as is practical.

The hearing aid was the first positive step toward what has been by turns my obsession and my disappointment. I wanted Charlie to speak. I understood about the utility and the beauty of sign language. I have never berated it. But, I needed to hear Charlie say, "Mama." I believe that speech allows the deaf greater freedom and independence in the world. Even the sign for a person who hears is *speak*, not *hear*. I felt then that we had made a start with the hearing aid. I believed speech would develop soon. Mercifully, I did not know then how slow, how laborious the process of teaching Charlie to speak would be. Neither did I know that he had been speaking to me all along, in ways I had ignored because they were different and required more effort.

3

It was not long after the discovery of Charlie's deafness that I began to study sign language. The decision to use the total communication method of teaching language (meaning the use of sign language, speech, and speechreading simultaneously) was certainly the easiest decision I made during those early months. When we came to live with my parents, even I could see how much Charlie and I relied upon gestures to communicate. It was something that had developed quite naturally during our long months alone. Abandoning the only communication that really worked for us in favor of the rigors of strict oral training seemed unreasonable. I could not begin again with a new system. So, the sign language training began.

As soon as a class was available, I enrolled. Betty asked to join me, and the rest of the family looked to us for instruction. Two nights a week, Betty and I took turns driving to class.

At the first session of the sign language class, introductions were made. Betty and I were the only ones who had regular contact with a deaf person. Some of the other students were interested in sign language as part of their special education training, and some worked with an occasional deaf client or customer. One older woman was losing her own hearing and was preparing herself with an alternative form of communication. My initial reaction was one of great pride. Surely these others would admire us for our determination to learn how to teach Charlie. Since ours seemed the most immediate need, I often monopolized the class with questions about signs for specific child-related activities. Looking back, the others were the admirable ones. I was there not by choice but by necessity. My child would be learning another language, so I had to learn it first. These others could have carried on without ever knowing a sign. Theirs was a more altruistic interest. Mine was basic survival, which hardly deserved admiration.

After each class, I brought home the new signs to my parents. We all learned together; it was an exciting time. Learning sign language was my first step toward accepting Charlie's handicap. I had heard the sad stories of hearing parents who do not learn to sign to their deaf children. These are not the strict oralists but parents who are waiting for their children to learn to communicate with them. I could not wait. The support of my entire family in these efforts was incalculable. We were taking ourselves to Charlie. For the first time, we were entering his world, not trying to drag him into ours. I have never regretted the decision to use sign language.

Charlie began to change. I don't mean that he began to read signs or to use them himself. That was to come only after more months of seemingly unrewarded effort. The difference is difficult to describe. The outbursts of frustration from both of us continued, but even he seemed to sense the hope of understanding and responded by being calmer, happier, and more confident.

At this point, we were teaching Charlie a sign as soon as we learned it. Every object, every person had a name—ball, chair, Mama. Each time an object came into Charlie's hand, I tried to give him the name, both the word and the sign. Of course, it was only effective if he were looking at me. It may not have been surprising that Charlie was usually more interested in getting his hands on a toy or drink than he was in watching for its name, but it was frustrating.

The sheer logistics of holding an object and trying to sign sometimes meant defeat. (If you are holding an object, you cannot always make the sign. So, you put it down to make the sign.) Once an object was out of my hand, Charlie would snatch it up. His eyes never left it to wander to my hands or face. Now, assuming by some great stroke of luck that Charlie did see the sign, for him to repeat it, he had to put down the object. Afraid he might lose it (children are also suspicious), Charlie would hold fast to his prize, giving me a full-face blank stare. While his attention was caught, I'd give the sign again. To make sure he understood the sign went with the object, I'd point to it. Then, with his eyes and hands both on the object, he was most likely to turn around and walk out of the room.

Charlie did learn to imitate signs fairly quickly. He is a natural mime, if anything is truly natural. I remember with a smile the first time I saw him pantomiming the actions of driving a car. He was playing by himself and I happened to walk in on him. He was walking about the room, his hands outstretched in front of him, grasping a steering wheel, which he turned most vigorously. He walked a few steps and stopped. He would then look in one direction or another and turn the wheel, following through with the turn. Sometimes, he checked behind before walking backwards.

I was amazed. It was obvious what he was doing, even though the gestures were conservative. He repeated each maneuver in precisely the same way each time. But, the look on his face was the best. His imagination was working full force. He was expressing with his hands and his body what was going on wordlessly in his mind. At two years old, he was communicating something more than a survival need—for the first time. To be sure, there must have been more vivid images in that head than all the most accomplished mimes could perform. He was enjoying his communication with himself, and I was enchanted watching him.

I wanted so much to get into his communication some way. I wanted to tell him that I knew what he meant and that I liked it, too. I started my imaginary car and joined him. At first, he looked puzzled. This was not the mouth moving or the pointing his mother usually engaged in. But, he accepted the attempt to communicate with a good spirit, and we both drove around that basement room in silence, but in understanding.

Charlie's prowess as a mime kept pace with his growth. As the years passed, he added all kinds of embellishments to his driving—turning the key, opening and closing the door, backing out, using the windshield wipers, scraping off the ice from the invisible glass, and (I confess with chagrin) smoking a cigarette. He added passengers, usually one of my parents or me. We were picked up and usually helped into our seats. Then, with Charlie in front and his passengers behind, we would walk through the house to a destination known only to the silent driver. Sometimes we were left in a distant part of the house, but more often we were brought back to our starting position. Then, with a smile and a wave, Charlie would drive on to his next fare.

To the cars, he has added school buses and city buses (on the latter you have to pay), trucks, and golf carts. One can tell the difference in subtle ways; how the door opens, how fast you go, the tilt of the steering wheel, how high one must step up into the cab. A keen observer, Charlie sometimes wears sunglasses or listens to the radio when he drives. In winter he occasionally has trouble getting up a hill, his tires spin a bit. He does all this without any props save his imagination. I don't always understand completely where I am to sit. I have been corrected for sitting on what must have been the hood of the car. Sometimes, I forget to close my door. Charlie usually rolls his eyes or, if I'm very slow, shakes his finger and reaches across to close it for me.

I sometimes thought that Charlie's rides were a way of communicating more than just the driving behavior he had observed in others. For one thing, his passengers never knew where they were going. A ride could last from one living room chair to the next. Or, it could take many passes through the house. That's how it was when Charlie rode in the car, only it was real. He never knew where he was going either. Maybe he accepted that as being the normal state of things. Even now, when he has much more language to draw on, he doesn't reveal the destination of an imaginary ride unless asked, and not always then. Maybe it was never a big question for him. Maybe the ride was enough. But, he must have wondered, at least on one occasion, where he was likely to wind up.

We take for granted that we know something about what is going to happen to us. It gives us some measure of control over ourselves and our environment. Did Charlie have some way of reading clues in a situation that told him what was happening? Or, for so long not knowing, had he resigned himself to frequent mysteries? I shall have to add these to the growing list of questions I want to ask Charlie when he grows up. When we can sit down and talk and I can get to know him. When he has the language to tell me about himself.

The process of learning sign language began when Charlie was about twenty months old. It continued, either in class or at home, all the time. Charlie imitated the signs he was given, but not always with meaning. If I said *water* and then he said *water*, it didn't necessarily mean he wanted water. It would be nearly a year before spontaneous signing would come. A whole year of seeming failure, or at least of little perceivable success.

Our daily communication at this stage centered around eating, a high-priority activity for any two-year-old. Mealtimes were not much of a problem. If carried to a table set with food, seated, and bibbed, Charlie understood it was time to eat. Likewise, if someone had food, whether eating it or preparing it, he was able to get the attention of whoever had the food or drink that he wanted. If offered (as it nearly always is to a small child), food can be either accepted or rejected without words. The more difficult situations were those times when Charlie wanted something that was not in open view. Possibly as a result of a lifetime of being incommunicado, Charlie usually attempted to fulfill his own needs before going through the trial and error process of trying to get what he wanted from someone else. Rummaging through a drawer, emptying a cabinet, or climbing on a table were the most direct ways of procuring for himself whatever it was he sought.

I found Charlie on any number of occasions perched precariously on a chair or table, reaching for something as tempting as a can of tomato paste. He would assure me most resolutely that he wanted tomato paste, or vinegar, or some other equally unlikely viand. It was then necessary to try and convince Charlie that cornstarch would not be much of a treat. I would try to divert his attention by offering bananas or crackers, even candy instead. But he'd stand firm. I would end up with a whole counter littered with items I was trying to push on an unyielding customer. I would point to the item Charlie thought he wanted and sign, "Bad, no good." "Not for little boys," I'd grimace. He'd laugh and grimace back. "Ah, he understands," I'd think. "I'll just return the chili seasoning to the back of the cabinet." Just then, Charlie would grab for it. I'd open the can and show Charlie how unappetizing green onion tops can be. "Yes, that's what I want," his face would say. Fine. I'd give him a spoonful of dry pinto beans to taste. No, this wasn't what he wanted. We'd start again.

Assuming we were fortunate enough to establish what Charlie wanted (for example, a drink), trying to define which drink put us back on square one again. A glass of water, when refused, would turn into a glass of milk. Sometimes, a whole row of little glasses resulted. Sometimes the sink filled with rejections. Desperation even drove me, once or twice, to let him sample from the orange juice carton or the soda bottle.

Sometimes food was cooked and served before it was rejected. Keep in mind that Charlie had no nods of the head for yes or no. Rejection could only come at the final moment when a freshly boiled hot dog was abandoned.

The first victim in this trial and error process of satisfying Charlie's hunger or thirst was usually my patience. "Can't you make up your mind what you want? Hurry up." Charlie's expression was one of fear, "I've upset her again. All I wanted was water." On other occasions, Charlie's patience would go first and a raging tantrum would ensue. In the end, we would both be shouting, slamming things around, and crying. When things would finally settle down and Charlie either had what he wanted or had given up, what remained was a mess in the kitchen and on me. I sensed that Charlie understood how helpless I was. I hope someday he can tell me how he felt. I wonder if he remembers these episodes with anger or with pity toward me. It was, after all, I who did not understand. Yes, he took a sip of wine once. I think frustration can cloud the judgment.

4

Charlie was approaching his second birthday. We had had four months of deafness. (I wonder how much of that time was wasted through my inability to cope.) I had begun to take some positive steps for Charlie and myself.

Alice, the audiologist from Dr. Whitaker's office, had told me about a former classmate of hers who was now a speech pathologist at a local hospital. Alice suggested that I contact her friend to get some advice and to possibly set up some private speech therapy sessions for Charlie. I did contact the therapist, and she agreed to see Charlie once or twice a week.

I took Charlie to his first speech therapy session because I wanted to meet the therapist and personally introduce her to Charlie. Betty took Charlie to the rest of his sessions, of which there were about a dozen. My main reason for sending Charlie to a speech therapist was to introduce him to the concept of words. I also thought it would be a good idea for him to get experience watching a teacher's face. He was almost two—the magic age when he became eligible for preschool.

I learned a lot from the materials the therapist gave me; Charlie got a taste of formal learning before actually starting school. He gave no outward sign of learning, but at least I had a chance to see him ignore someone besides me. My assignment during this period was to find a preschool for Charlie. It only took a few telephone calls to discover that the only game in town was the Crippled Children's Nursery School (wouldn't I ever get away from that word—*crippled*). The school was a private preschool for children with all types of physical handicaps. The school had one class for hearing-impaired children.

At last, Charlie was ready for school. With my sign language class and Charlie's speech therapy sessions behind us, I felt we were well prepared for Charlie's formal education. I should have been accustomed to being wrong by this time, but I was even wrong about that. Once again, the goddess of motherhood had turned her back on me. Bad weather and a bad case of the flu delayed Charlie's enrollment nearly a month. Panic gripped me as I contemplated the limited facilities available for children his age with his handicap. What if they gave his place to a child whose mother was capable of keeping him or her healthy? I called the director of the preschool. She had trouble hiding the humor in her voice. ("Hey, I got another hysterical mother here, close the door.") She assured me that there would be a place for Charlie when he was well.

I went to visit the school with Charlie a few days before he was to begin. Everything was wonderful. The facilities and the staff were excellent. All great. But, from the moment I crossed the threshold, I felt stupid, inept, and generally a failure. Here were people doing with ease what I was struggling so to learn. They were signing and talking effortlessly, and at the same time. With me, I could hardly keep mouth and hands together. I was like an old movie out of sync. No wonder Charlie didn't pay more attention to me than he did. I probably made him dizzy.

First, we were given a tour. Charlie followed along behind me, tugging at my arm just enough to make me keep pulling. In one hallway we saw little coats hung low on the wall, each below a printed name.

"The children must hang up their own coats when they come in from the bus or the playground. They soon learn to recognize their own hooks, and seeing the cards helps them recognize their names," the director explained.

Charlie did not take off his own coat at home, but other two-year-olds obviously did. Charlie would have been just as content to leave his coat on in the house all the time. To a kid who could tolerate wet pants (and worse), a coat was no big deal. I decided these kids probably had help with their coats.

"Of course, their teachers help them with their coats. (See!) Then, they walk together to their classroom."

In the classroom for hearing-impaired children, I met Charlie's new teacher. Trying to pry a clinging Charlie from behind my knees while donning a humiliated half-smile, I introduced myself. (Great opening. The teacher already knows that you have lost control.) The teacher seemed incredibly young, or I incredibly old. Several years my junior, she and an even younger aide were keeping five toddlers quietly occupied.

"This is Charlie? At last. Is he feeling better?" she asked.

"Yes, thank you."

"Let me see you, Charlie." As she gently pulled Charlie from beneath my coat, I tried to shove him, but discreetly.

"Hi," she signed. "My name is Cathy. What's your name?" Charlie stared at her.

"What's his name sign?" Cathy asked me.

(Good God. He doesn't have one.) "Well, I guess he really doesn't have one yet. We've only started to sign."

"Well, let's see. We have one *C* already. My name sign is a *C* on the shoulder. How about *C* on the temple? Do you like that, Charlie? Your name is Charlie," she said as she signed it.

Just like that. Within fifteen seconds she had named him. I had had him for two years, nameless. Or at least name-signless. I began to feel that familiar rush of nauseating stupidity. I later (much later) learned that Charlie's name sign is very close to one of the signs for *sunshine*. I tell people he's my sunshine boy. It's stupid, I know, but less so than admitting he was given his name sign by a complete stranger.

Cathy went through some of the class activities for me and explained how they used signs and spoken language in all of them. "We do most of the same things any preschool does; we just pay more attention to language learning." I noticed several large mirrors and commented on them.

"We use mirrors a lot. Have you held Charlie up to one and encouraged him to imitate your mouth movements?" I had not.

"Yes. I read that in the John Tracy Clinic material." A little lie. I would begin using the mirror. Tonight.

"Oh, you have the John Tracy books?" A small point for me to begin to atone for the name business. The John Tracy Clinic course for parents is designed to give suggestions and guidance to parents working at home with their own deaf child. It is sent out in units over a year's time, but really continues to be used throughout a child's language-learning years. There are periodic reports to be completed by the parents. These reports are answered on an individual basis by a member of the clinic staff and the responses are most encouraging and helpful.

"Yes, well, I've just started the course, but I do try to do the games with Charlie."

"That's good. It's so important to work with Charlie all the time. We only have him a few hours a week, so much of his language must be learned at home. Have you taken a sign language course?"

"Yes. So has my sister-in-law. She's Charlie's second mother, while I work."

"That's great. It sounds like you've made a good start." Charlie was back behind my knees again, so her praise rang a little hollow.

"He's a little shy," I apologized.

"Of course. It's all new to him. He'll be fine."

We talked a bit more, and Charlie wandered off to play with some blocks. I asked about the little cards taped to various objects around the room—*chair*, *table*, *door*, all labeled.

"Those are to help the children with the concept that objects have names. It helps in reading readiness, too. Some of the children are a little older than Charlie, and we want them to be ready for kindergarten next year. John Tracy Clinic suggests these labels."

"I must not have gotten to that lesson yet." Awash in my inadequacy, I vowed to label everything in the house that very night.

As Cathy's answers to my persistent questions became shorter and shorter, I sensed her desire to return to her students. They had all, by now, joined Charlie in scattering blocks all over the floor. Cathy asked the aide to escort me back to the director's office while she tried to salvage her classroom.

The director guided Charlie and me through the other rooms at the school: the physical therapy room, the speech therapy room, and the play room. I watched for Charlie's reaction, expecting that he would squeal with delight at his newest experience and refuse to leave when the time came. He did not. At two years, he failed to understand the importance of his education in terms of his future as an independent person. Here he would begin his acquisition of communication. He would learn life skills and how to cope with a hearing world. He would make friends and learn to feel his worth as a person who is deaf. Charlie did not, of course, recognize any of this significance. He saw strangers only. He did not even understand that he would be coming back here again, alone, so he urged our departure. I lingered, asking questions. The director seemed not as impressed with me as I had hoped.

"Oh yes, we all sign at home."

"That is great. Do you also sign when you are talking to each other? When Charlie is *listening?*"

"Well, no. We've only recently started, but I know it is important that he be included in as much as possible." (Mea culpa, mea culpa, mea maxima culpa.)

"Is Charlie potty trained?"

"Well, not yet. It's been a little difficult getting that started what with my working. And his communication problem, of course. How do you bribe someone whose language sophistication is confined to the immediate present?"

"You could show him the reward. Nothing quite so immediate as what's before your eyes."

"Does Charlie have to be potty trained before he can start school?" (Charlie, you have exactly one hour, so get trained!)

"No. You can send a box of disposable diapers, and we'll let you know when he's running low. I think we may have another little one or two in diapers yet. Being around other children will help Charlie to catch on more quickly, I'm sure." (Rough translation: If you were a *good* mother, you would have him trained already.)

"Did Cathy give you a sign language book?"

"Yes, but I . . ."

"Good. That's only a beginning. I know you'll want to get enrolled in a regular sign language class right away."

"I've taken one semester at night."

"Excellent. Then you've made a good start. Home support makes our job so much easier." (Funny, I thought good schools made my job easier.)

"Now, you'll want Charlie to ride the bus?"

"Yes."

"All right. I'll have to talk to the driver who has your route and find out what time you'll need to meet the bus. I assume that since you work, someone else will meet the bus when we bring him home at noon."

"My sister-in-law Betty will be keeping Charlie. I'll ask her."

"Now, it's important that she be there every day. If no authorized person is there, that means someone you've told us about in advance, we have to bring Charlie back to school and call you to pick him up."

"That is no problem. I have a very supportive family, one of us will always be there."

More questions. More answers. Charlie, by now, had discovered the wonderland of toys in the director's office and was not eager to leave. I was beginning to wish that he were so I could have an excuse to go. I was feeling a bit shaky. Charlie was beginning to grab things on the director's desk and wander off with them into her secretary's office. I tried to retrieve him and laughed rather sheepishly at his restlessness. The director assured me that it was all right for him to explore. There was nothing he could hurt. Still, I felt rather that she was tolerating his behavior because she sensed my incompetence to correct it. I think now that it was a mistake to feel so responsible for Charlie's every action. Once a child leaves your body, you have lost control, and you can never get it back.

"One question," I said, "then I really must get back to work (that wonderful excuse). Do your hearing-impaired children learn to talk?"

I sensed a stifled sigh. "We have individual speech therapy with each child every day. I'm sure you work on speech at home. With new techniques and equipment, the potential for speech in a child like Charlie is good. But, it always depends on the motivation of the individual child. Some children, usually boys, learn speech more slowly. You can do a lot toward helping Charlie learn to speak." (What if I can't?)

I left in a cloud of "thank yous" with the director repeating "everything will be fine" and "he'll soon adjust to school," and several mutual offers to "call me any time."

I made many promises to myself as we drove back home in silence. Since Charlie had not yet learned much sign language nor to watch me in the rearview mirror, our car rides were usually pretty quiet. I smiled to myself at the thought that I was doing something good and positive for Charlie by enrolling him in preschool. It was only two mornings a week, but it was a beginning. And, it was obvious. Anyone viewing my performance in this situation (and I was convinced nearly everyone in a four-state radius was doing just that) would have to agree that I had made a sensible, well-reasoned decision for my son. There was more I should be doing, such as using the mirrors, the labels, and so on, and I would do it all, too.

Looking back, I notice that most of my feelings about Charlie's launch into education concerned myself. My happiness, my gratefulness, my pride. I did feel fortunate to have found a good preschool for Charlie. But, what were his feelings? Remember that we are dealing with a time when Charlie had only rudimentary communication. After only a few weeks of hesitant signing

47

at home and several fifteen-minute sessions with a speech therapist, our working vocabulary consisted of gestures, pantomime, misunderstanding, and almost constant frustration. He had no inkling that this short visit was only the first of many trips to school. How could he? How could I tell him?

School started not with a bang or a whimper but with sobs. The morning came for Charlie's first day. For him, nothing was different. He was awake with a smile at our usual ridiculously early hour. Even his new jeans, which had a real zipper instead of an elastic waistband, did not impress him as being the landmark in his development that I had intended. Charlie must have sensed my tension that morning for I hurried him more mercilessly than usual. With coat collar pulled up and hat pulled down, he had to hold his head up awkwardly in order to see out the small slit I had left him. His coat and snow pants were so thick that he could barely bend at the knees, and so he made his way down the driveway stiff-legged with arms outstretched.

We did not drive to Betty's house that morning. As soon as I backed the car out of the driveway, preparing to turn in the opposite direction, Charlie knew something different was happening. He looked at me with a questioning face. "Where this time?" There was absolutely no way for me to tell him where we were going or what was about to happen. For Charlie, every car ride was a mystery. Would he ride for five minutes or for five hours? Where would he end up? He never knew in those days, and I couldn't tell him. I had, of course, shown Charlie pictures of a school bus. We had driven by the parking lot where the local school buses were parked so Charlie could see them. I had shown him a picture of a school bus just before we left the house that morning. No doubt he thought we were going to see one again. He could not have dreamed that he was about to ride in one all by himself. I could not prepare him by explaining that Betty would be there to pick him up. I could not bribe him with the hope that he could have a special treat if he were a good boy. It would all be new. All thrown at him at once with no way for me to ease the fear. I ached for him.

We were to meet the school bus in the parking lot of a church. When we arrived, Charlie wanted to get out of the car and go inside the building. Perhaps he thought it was a store with toys inside. I would not let him out of the car. His face begged me for an explanation, but it was impossible to give one. It was a cold February day, and I kept the car running—another oddity for Charlie. I could see anxiety spreading over the part of his tiny face that was visible. I signed "bus" and pointed to him. I showed him the picture and, using my fingers to represent Charlie, walked up to the bus to ride.

I was afraid, too. I'm sure Charlie sensed it. Perhaps it was my own fear that I saw reflected in his face. I don't really know. Perhaps someday Charlie will tell me how he felt, if he still remembers.

The bus came. It stopped and the gaping mouth of its doors opened, ready to swallow up my frightened child. Other parents got out of cars around us and took their children up to the bus. Some wore braces. One little girl walked unsteadily on miniature crutches. The preschool included classes for children with all types of handicaps. I felt a difference between the other parents and me. Their children could at least be comforted by their reassurances. Mine could not. Charlie's eyes widened as he took in all that was happening. Putting on my most confident face, I carried him to the door of the bus. The driver was friendly and quite comfortable with the special passengers she carried. Some drooped helplessly in their seats. Others sat bolt upright, their backs braced.

"Is this Charlie?"

"Yes. Hello."

"What a beautiful little boy. With a face like that he should have been a little girl. Put him up front so he can watch me," she suggested. Charlie began to cry as I fastened his seat belt. "Don't worry. They always cry the first few times. He'll be just fine," the bus driver told me.

I was sure that he would be. I knew he was in capable hands and that all of this was right and good, but it did not stop the lump from rising in my own throat. I turned away abruptly and left him sobbing and screaming. I walked back to my own car and waited until the bus pulled away. Only the top of Charlie's little head was visible through the window. It bobbed right along with the other kids' as the bus moved. I cried aloud as I followed the bus for the stretch of road we both traveled. The sign on the bus identified that these were handicapped children, and my child was right there with them. The sign might as well have been around Charlie's neck, I thought.

Why was I crying? Because Charlie was so vulnerable, all alone in that bus? Because I was sending him off to a frightening experience for which I could not prepare him? Because he was going to begin his association with other deaf children? He was going to discover his own world for the first time. I would never have all of him back again. He would discover in his deaf friends things that I could never give him, and my inadequacy was overwhelming just then. I felt for the first time that we were truly different from each other and that there were parts of him I would never understand. There would be feelings and experiences that he would have to find in his own world, and he would not be able to bring them back to share with me.

The bus rides became less traumatic with time. By the end of the school year, Charlie was actually enjoying them. However, not wanting me to get out of this completely guilt-free, he found a way to express his displeasure with me. Each morning that we met the bus, which at first was only twice a week, Charlie soiled his diaper (I believe that is the current euphemism). Potty training was not progressing as I had hoped, but at least this particular function was predictable, if less than convenient. Each time it happened, I crawled gracelessly into the back seat of my subcompact car to make the necessary cleanup. Satisfied that he had made his point, Charlie boarded the bus for a morning of learning and fun. I rode to work with the great equalizer. On one most unfortunate occasion, I left the item in my car all day long. After that, I opted for the more embarrassing, if less odiferous, alternative of taking it into the building where I worked for proper disposal. So, each Tuesday and Thursday morning I strode into work and headed directly for the ladies' room, there to rid myself of what I hoped others took to be a paper bag containing the beginning of the digestive chain—of all things, my lunch.

After Charlie started school, the reality of our separation sat heavy on me. No mother can deny some sadness at her child's advancements. It signals her own aging and the inevitability of someday losing what was once part of her own body. In Charlie's case, though, the separation was more than that of a child progressing to independence. It was the admission that he was not like me. Normally hearing two-year-olds do not often ride a bus by themselves to a preschool an hour's distance from home. There are always closer resources for them. Charlie's opportunities were restricted to a limited number of locations. It's true that almost every state has a residential school for the deaf, but would I have to move to put Charlie in one of them? I realized that from now on, my opportunities would be restricted, too.

Charlie's separation from me revealed itself in another way. I could not ask him about his day at school. *What did you do? What did you eat for a snack? Did you play outside?* were beyond his comprehension. It would be years before Charlie's language progressed to that conversational level. I relied on his teacher to keep me informed. This she did most cooperatively, of course, but it was not possible for me to talk with her every day. She did write me notes as her time permitted. But, two-and-a-half hours go by quickly for someone trying to manage toddlers.

I did not know, for instance, that Charlie liked graham crackers. He had never eaten them for me at home, so I stopped buying them. There was no, "I had graham crackers at school and they were real good," to let me know his changing food tastes. I was left out and felt it.

I kept in close contact with Charlie's teacher in an effort to reinforce at home what he was learning at school. It was challenging to plan games and learning experiences for Charlie. A teacher by training and by inclination (if not by profession), I had been given the most important student of all. My zealousness in teaching Charlie was genuine, if not always productive.

51

One of the activities Charlie's teacher told me about was a game they played to help the children listen for sounds they could hear. We played the game at home, with marginal success at first, but later with amazing results. Charlie was asked to hold a small flag. He then turned his back to me. I held a drum (in our case, an empty coffee can with a plastic lid) and a wooden spoon. Charlie's job was to wave the flag whenever he heard the sound of the drum. Then, of course, he had to turn around for applause and praise. Having once learned the game, his responses were correct nearly every time, even when I hesitated before giving him the beat. I could have played the game for hours, the results were that good and good results came so rarely then. But, a few waves and it was my turn to be the listener. So, I dutifully stood with my back to him. He would beat the can a few times and praise me for my good responses. Everyone in the family took a turn, as Charlie alternated between student and teacher. Then, when he was satisfied that we had all done well, he would leave the drum and the flag to play his own version of the game. I tried not to overdo the game, so he would not become bored with it and resist, but I confess that the sight of that flag waving to the beat of my three-pound, mountain-grown noisemaker outdid any Fourth of July parade ever staged.

Charlie's teacher had also suggested that I find out about the John Tracy Clinic home course for parents. How proud I was to tell her that I had already enrolled and had received the first lessons. When my first lesson arrived, I read through it quickly. Here would be the formula, the step-by-step instructions on how to teach Charlie to speak and to sign. I encouraged everyone in the family to read the material. I even organized a card file of learning games. All joined in enthusiastically.

One suggestion for learning speechreading and speech (John Tracy Clinic uses the oral approach; add signs for total communication) was the surprise box.

> The box should be filled with simple objects. Bring out the closed box with an aura of mystery. "What is inside? Let's see." Then, with your child seated attentively in front of you, bring out one object at a

time. Name it and use the name in several short phrases.

Charlie's job in all of this seemed simple enough. He was to watch my face. After the surprise of pulling out a new object, his eyes were supposed to go immediately to my face so they could drink in the language. At least, that is the way the game is described. I wrote it all out, including the suggested items for the surprise box, on one of my game file cards. What John Tracy Clinic told me, but what I disbelieved, was that the child has to learn to look at the parent's face. I assumed that this lifting of the eyes, hungrily, to the speaker's face was some sort of instinctual behavior the deaf were given as a compensation for their lack of hearing. Mother Nature is not so generous. Face-watching must be learned. It must be learned before speechreading and before talking. John Tracy Clinic told me it would take a very long time to teach Charlie to watch my face. It took weeks and months.

First attempt: I pulled out a little ball. "Ball," I said. "I have a ball. See my ball." Charlie grabbed the ball, got up, and left the room with it. My carefully packed surprise box and I sat ignored on the floor.

> Keep the objects in the box new and exciting. Change some of them each time, but repeat items periodically for reinforcement.

Second attempt: I sat down on the living room floor with Charlie. I showed him the box and wrestled him into a sitting position opposite me. "What do I have?" I began. The first object out of the box was a shoe. "This is a shoe. Do you have a shoe? See my shoe," I said in my most expressive face. Charlie got up, went to his room, got the ball from the first attempt, and put it in the box. I persisted with the shoe until he grabbed the ball back out of the box and left.

> Use the same box so that the child can identify it and knows that the game is about to begin. He will soon learn what his role is in the game and will sit down eager to play.

Third attempt: I brought the box out of the bedroom and headed for the living room floor. Charlie saw me in the hall, recognized the box, grabbed it, and dumped it out. Picking out the toys he wanted, he strolled off.

> Don't force the child to sit longer than his attention span will allow. When he is finished, tell him it was a good job and let him help put things away.

Sixth attempt: We had mastered the steps of sitting on the floor opposite each other. Charlie waited for me to open the box and take out the first object. "Here is the ball. A big ball." Charlie looked directly at the ball. I went through the entire box (about four items) and he never once glanced toward my face. Still he sat, waiting for more objects. We put the objects back into the box. One by one, I talked about each, then gave the toy to Charlie to put in the box. His eyes had not yet moved away from the toy. I took the objects out of the box a second time. This time, I held each one provocatively in front of my face. Charlie was nearly cross-eyed from looking squarely at the object without once seeing my face. He continued to sit, ready now to put the toys back into the box. Bored with the game, I tossed the toys into the box and walked out of the room with it.

> Wait for a response. Don't give the object to the child until he has looked at your face, however briefly. Keep hold of it, and the child, feeling you will not let go, will look at your face.

Tenth attempt: I took the toy boat out of the box. "This is a boat. It is a blue boat. Do you want the boat?" No response, no watching the face. Charlie reached for the boat, but I held onto it. I waited for him to look up. By now I was pulling back on the boat to keep from losing it. Still no look. Now, we were in a tug-of-war over the boat, and Charlie was squealing with delight. Determined to wait for a response, I held fast. Charlie let go and I fell back, hitting my head on a chair. Charlie came over, stared into my face, and then burst into hysterical laughter. He took the next object out of the box and handed it to me, ready for another tug-of-war. It would be many days before the eleventh attempt at the surprise box.

I did try other learning games with varying degrees of success. At first my plans were too elaborate. By the time I had finished demonstrating what Charlie was to do, he had either dropped off to sleep or left the room. Many times, I was abandoned with a carefully arranged set of objects and a bowl of M & M's. Therapists sometimes use M & M's as a reward with very young children. A good technique, when used in moderation. Charlie, of course, was completely uninterested in the M & M's and never ate them. I usually found them later, on the sole of my shoe or in the pockets of his pants as I removed them from the dryer. M & M's may not melt in your hand, but they bloody well can't take a dryer.

John Tracy Clinic and Charlie's teacher encouraged reading to him as a language-building activity. After discovering Charlie's deafness, I had called a temporary moratorium on reading. I remembered my early attempts to read to Charlie. Unaware of his handicap, I had seated him on my lap with a book for quiet time. I felt very good about the way this felt and looked. It could have been a scene from "Donna Reed" or "Leave It to Beaver," the ideal families I grew up with. I read the stories to Charlie in my most dramatic voices, pointing out the action in the pictures. How stupid I felt later to think of those early story times. Charlie's back had been to me, so he had seen nothing but my hands pointing at pictures and turning pages. After Charlie's deafness was diagnosed, I thought I would have to wait for story time until Charlie could read to himself, and I wondered how I would hold a ten-year-old on my lap.

Assured by the experts that reading stories was an important part of learning, I attacked the problem in truly creative ways. I set Charlie on my lap facing me with the book between us. This meant I had to either read upside down or keep flipping the book around. Then, there was the problem of keeping the pages open while I signed. Imagine the scene: a smallish mother, child facing her perched precariously on the tips of her knees; she holds a book open with her elbows while signing. No wonder

Charlie wouldn't sit still for it. He was falling off my knees laughing at me.

Next, we tried sitting opposite each other at a table with the book propped on a box or bowl between us. At some point, the prop holding the book would slip and that would end the story. Reading made the surprise box look like a howling success. Charlie was expected to look at the book and then at me, to keep his hands off the book, and to copy my signs. He was also expected to enjoy himself. All of this proved too taxing for both of us. I usually ended the story on page three, giving the book to Charlie to peruse at will. I tried to interject a word or two as the pictures flew past. Possibly the biggest achievement at this time was that Charlie did not try to eat the book or throw it at me.

I tried on a few occasions to act out stories for Charlie without the obstacle of a book. I felt that introducing him to the children's classics through mime was of great cultural benefit to him. I worried that Charlie would grow up culturally deprived of the fantasy friends familiar to most children through the miracle of the mass media.

For my first performance, Charlie sat in the big rocking recliner in the living room. His feet stuck straight out in front of him in the big chair and he tapped his toes together continuously. I stood center stage in the middle of the room. Charlie tried several times to get out of the chair until I forced him to sit down and stay there. Threatened with sitting in the chair or going to bed for the rest of the year, he became a most captive audience. In my halting signs (even though I practiced the story in front of the bathroom mirror), I began. I had chosen the story of the three bears because it was free of the troublesome names that plague children's stories. Rapunsel and Humpty Dumpty may be delightful on the ear of a hearing child, but fingerspelling them repeatedly throughout a story is very tiresome. I began.

"One time there were three bears." I had a teddy bear to clarify beyond a doubt the sign for bear.

"A daddy bear," (teddy held high in the air) " a mama bear, " (teddy held even with my height) "and a baby bear" (teddy cradled in my arms).

"The three bears lived in a big house. In the house were three chairs. A big chair—SIT DOWN CHARLES AND WATCH—a middle chair, and a little chair." By now there was also a rocking reclining chair, for Charlie had left the room.

During Charlie's first year in preschool, we all worked very hard to learn how to teach him language. The whole family was involved, but it was a gruelingly slow process. For children who can hear, language acquisition is basically a passive activity. They receive input constantly from what they hear around them whether they happen to be paying attention or not. As a language teacher, I knew that a learner must hear (or see) many repetitions of a word before it is mastered sufficiently to be used comfortably and easily in a conversational vocabulary. For a hearing child, these repetitions may be accomplished without much effort. The child is not really aware of the process. Any mother who wonders where her little darling "picked up such language" should give her child's surroundings a listen.

For deaf children these repetitions must be given to them when they are fully attentive. In very young children, this means that sufficient repetitions for mastery of a single word may take weeks. Language builds on itself. New words cannot be added until the earlier concepts have been learned. This makes the process of teaching language to a deaf child seem interminable in the early stages.

My family and I spent weeks training Charlie to watch the speaker's face. More weeks passed before he began imitating our signs. Months passed when he seemed to stay at about the same level before he inched ahead again. The frustration was monstrous. Even after I had learned what we needed to do for Charlie, I simply could not make it happen. I lost my motivation on many occasions. In a sense, the frustration became worse after we started to work with Charlie. Before, his lack of response was excusable, or at least understandable. Now, all the opportunities to learn language seemed wasted on him.

We were not ignoring the little hearing Charlie did have. Efforts continued to train Charlie to use his residual hearing. A child profoundly deaf from birth learns to shut out meaningless noises. Unable to locate the source of sounds he heard or vibrations he felt, Charlie learned to tune them out. We all do the same thing. An apartment dweller learns to ignore the random sounds of living coming from the neighbors. A big part of preparing Charlie to learn language was encouraging him to open himself up to the visual and auditory cues that were available to him. Learning to pay attention to the sounds he could hear came only after several months' work.

As I mentioned earlier, during the first few months that I was learning sign language, I was trying to teach it to Charlie. This meant I had to stay ahead of situations and anticipate words I would need so I could look them up. Often, though, I found Charlie's attention caught by some object or activity whose sign I did not know. I'd dash to the dictionary to look it up, but when I'd return at last with the proper word, Charlie was either gone or involved in something different. Another opportunity lost. Perhaps the next one would not come for days.

As Charlie grew older, dictionaries presented another problem. After he started school he sometimes brought home new signs that I did not know. Sign language dictionaries are, generally, alphabetical listings of words with accompanying diagrams of the signs. Finding the meaning of a sign entails flipping through pictures until the proper diagram is located. At least one book I have is arranged by handshape, which helps, but it is also the book with the fewest signs, which doesn't. The problem is further complicated by the fact that young deaf children misform signs just as hearing children mispronounce spoken words. Even if I found the sign's diagram, it might not be quite the same as Charlie's version. Just as there is baby talk, there are baby signs.

In American Sign Language the names of cities and people must be spelled out. A name sign is used in conversation. Name signs are completely arbitrary and are assigned to each person within certain limited conventions. For instance, if you were to meet someone and he fingerspelled his name J-O-H-N

S-M-I-T-H, you would then ask his name sign so that you would not have to spell his name in its entirety each time it was used. Many people use their initials, which are generally signed on the chest, close to the face, or on the upper arm. There could be a lot of J.S.'s in the world, and the only way to know just who those initials stand for would be to spell the name out letter by letter. Now for John Smith this might not be so cumbersome. But, when someone's mother has the lack of foresight to name him Charles Montgomery Forecki, it is a bit overwhelming. I should say in my defense that when that name was given, I was thinking more about how it would look on a book cover or an executive office door than about the effort required to fingerspell such a handful.

Charlies's name sign (thanks to his first teacher) is a *C* at the temple. (The upper part of the head is used for male signs: *man, boy, father, grandfather*. The lower part of the face is for *woman, girl, mother, grandmother*.) Charlie will no doubt add the *F* to his name sign later, or he may change his name sign, moving it to another part of his body.

Proper nouns can be hair-pullers for novice signers, whether hearing or deaf. This is especially true because our culture is very product oriented. How do you find out if a young child wants an Oreo or a Twinkie when neither of these words exists in sign language? Older children and adults can spell what they want or use a home-made sign, but toddlers still struggling with "want eat" cannot. When a child can't name or describe what he or she wants, and when mother doesn't have a name for it either, confusion reigns. It may seem a petty grievance, but I can't tell you how many bowls of Rice Krispies were thrown out when it was Cheerios Charlie wanted. Have you ever tried to persuade a child to settle for Spaghettios when it's NoodleRoni on which she has set her breaking heart? Try telling a child fruit punch and Kool-Aid are chemically indistinguishable.

When Charlie developed more language, we were able to overcome this problem somewhat by inventing our own names for specific products. *White* crackers were, of course, saltines, as opposed to *brown* (graham) crackers. For breakfast, one could enjoy *three boy cereal* (Rice Krispies has three boys on the box). In one of my weaker moments at the supermarket, I let Charlie buy *bird cereal* (the Froot Loops symbol is a toucan). I took a perverse pleasure in asking Charlie if he wanted bird cereal when the supermarket aisle was crowded. It quickly became quiet enough to hear the canned music.

We also invented signs for TV shows. When Charlie sat down to watch TV, he always hoped for the *orange flying car*. This, naturally, was the universal Friday night babysitter, "The Dukes of Hazzard."

Deafness is an all-pervading handicap. It is more than the inability to hear sound. It is not being an active participant in one's own culture. There is an immaturity or a naivete associated with deaf children, which is not entirely misplaced. Certainly deaf children lag behind their hearing peers in many areas of social relations.

Knowing which child is the bully, who the liar, the selfish one, or the cry baby must come from personal observation by the deaf child or from experience. All children must learn to deal with different personalities. A deaf child is more easily conned. Not having heard the neighborhood gossip about some unsavory character, the deaf child may become an unwitting victim.

There have been children who would not play with Charlie. Since he couldn't understand the discussion about what to do, Charlie had to stand aside and watch for a while to see what the game was. Sometimes what he perceived the kids to be doing was not right at all, and sometimes he came in at the wrong turn. Other times, the children would agree to change the rules somewhat in the middle of the game. This left Charlie doing the wrong thing to the annoyance of the less tolerant. This was always extremely painful for me to watch without involving myself. (Hey, you let Charlie have a turn or I'll make him bring his $30.00 truck in the house.)

Once I heard a child say, "Let's go play somewhere else. Charlie can't play right." Another time it was, "Here comes

Charlie. Let's go to the back." I don't know which was more intense, my pain or my anger. There Charlie stood, alone, looking puzzled. After a moment, he simply followed after them. Naturally, he didn't know what had happened. I did, and the next time I saw the tricycle of that boorish child in question, I took the opportunity to kick it over. It felt great! These children have been rare, I admit, but I think we all know the kind of adults they grow up to be.

For a deaf youngster, anticipating upcoming events is very difficult. Charlie's grasp of the concept *later* was positively the greatest boon to our relationship. It allowed him to have some hope and to trust me. Before that, each minute held some anxiety because he was unable to understand what was going to happen next. He never knew when he woke up from his nap who would be in the house, if he would be going somewhere, or in what I might be involved. Even after Charlie learned to communicate well, these new situations could be a problem. "We are going to the store," could mean almost anywhere. We differentiated the stores by saying the food store, the ice cream store, and the duck store. This last one had a mechanical duck outside which could be ridden for twenty-five cents. You learn to use whatever works.

Several weeks after Charlie started school, a parents' meeting was called. Everything I had read or heard underscored the need for support groups, and certainly other parents of deaf children were the ideal group from which to get support. I went, of course, but primarily because it seemed like something I should do for Charlie. Any demonstrable show of my efforts made me feel less helpless, or more precisely, made me feel that other people saw me as less helpless. At this point, I still felt that my inability to cope with Charlie's handicap was common knowledge to everyone in the city. Therefore, any evidence I could show of positive action on my part ought to brighten my image. I confess to this being my primary motivation for going to the parents' meeting. But, I was not so utterly without substance not to want to learn something, too.

The parents at the meeting ran the gamut socially. Their children were also very different in terms of degree of hearing loss and communication development. Some children had been in preschool for some time and would soon be entering kindergarten. One boy's speech was quite good. His grandmother was very attentive and encouraged speech and signing from him. I made a mental note of all the children who were more advanced than Charlie. At the coffee break, I would check their audiograms on the back wall. Undoubtedly, their hearing losses were less severe than Charlie's.

I sat through the "coming together" portion of the meeting with all my defenses high. I felt that my work with Charlie was under scrutiny by these people and that his progress was disappointing compared to some. I rehearsed every one of my excuses in case someone would say to me, "Hello. I'm Timmy's mother. You must be Charlie's mom. My, you aren't doing nearly enough with him, are you? Look, he hardly communicates at all. What a shame that you are so lazy with him." Paranoia reached its all time high that night.

Then, the coup de grace. A family came in just as we were about to start the meeting. Two things were evident at once: the child was the class superstar and his parents were responsible. Everyone knew the child. I sensed almost a nod from the other parents. My eyes flew to Charlie to see if he would acknowledge the wunderkind. Mercifully, he did not. Charlie was as oblivious to this entrance as he was to everything else in the room, except maintaining his perch on my lap. With the arrival of the whiz kid, the other children who had been sticking pretty close to their parents left gleefully to follow their leader. On my Charlie clung. I took some minute degree of pleasure from the notion that Charlie was at least displaying some individuality. If he were not the leader, neither was he a sheep.

As I listened to the conversations around me, I quickly learned things which lessened somewhat the blow of meeting the Wonder Family. First, the child had two parents, a complete set, in contrast to Charlie's solitary one. Second, the mother did not have to work all day. That is how the two parents maintained what I saw to be nearly twenty-four-hour language instruction. I had to be away from Charlie during our most productive hours in order to provide for his survival. What good was a great vocabulary if a child was too weak from hunger to pronounce it? I felt somewhat nobler, then. This excuse firmly planted in my mind, I was prepared to defend the criticism I believed would be forthcoming—that I was not doing enough for my child.

Apart from the persecution I had directed at myself early in the evening, this meeting had been a good experience. I heard other parents talk about their problems in dealing with their child's handicap. Amazingly, we had some identical concerns. Except for the superchild business, I came away from the meeting feeling pretty good.

At the next parents' meeting, I resolved I would do better. What this "better" meant was that I would appear more confident and in control, even humor-filled, glad for this opportunity for Charlie and me to grow together. As the meeting began, I told myself that sharing his learning was the most rewarding thing I could do with my life. Apart, that is, from seeing that Charlie had food to eat and a place to live. This experience was opening new horizons for me. I was reaching an untapped potential. It was surprising that I was not able to take flight, right there in the meeting room, on the strength of my superlative character.

Probably the real reason for my confident approach to this meeting was the absence of the Wonder Family. In fact, I'm sure that is true because when I turned around and saw their entrance only seconds before the speaker began, there was a decided squirming as I attempted to disappear into my chair. Had my wings not been so unfurled from the previous minute's flight, I might have made it.

The program was about career education for deaf students. The message was optimistic, the presentation upbeat. By the third or fourth slide, however, I was in tears. For the first time I was facing the reality of Charlie's education. He would not be reading by the midterm of kindergarten. He would not be making oral book reports in second grade. His academic education would be slow and arduous. His reading level at high school graduation would be lower than twelfth grade. (It was sometime later when perspective had found its way back that I concluded the average public school graduate can boast little better.)

Emphasis at the school from which this speaker came was on preparation for life in a hearing world. I settled back. This sounded better, and I decided to pay attention. Many occupations are open to the deaf, and more are opening up all the time. With the exception of talking on a phone, there is virtually no job skill for which a deaf person cannot be trained. The gentleman making the presentation proceeded to enumerate occupations for which his school provided training: clerical, auto repair, welding, baking. The list was quite long. It was also well below what I had envisioned for my son. I waited for this portion of the presentation to end so that we could move on to high tech careers and the professions. But, the slide show ended before the speaker got that far. The lights came on and questions were encouraged. Hands hesitantly went up around me, but I blurted out my plaintive question, "Don't any of your students go to college?"

Perhaps it was my tone—disbelief mixed with a hint of desperation. At any rate, I was the object of many stares and even an occasional gaping mouth. "Oh, come on," I thought. "You surely can't expect Super Kid back there to be a welder. No? Then not my child either. Had he been hearing, he would have been a bilingual classical musician engineer. Now, you want me to look forward to being the mother of a baker's helper."

I'm not sure what the school administrator said. Probably something about Gallaudet College in Washington, D.C., and the National Technical Institute for the Deaf in New York. There was, undoubtedly, some mention made of realistic expectations and surely he added that new opportunities were being made available every year. I do remember, quite distinctly, a comment on the importance of parental reinforcement of the school's efforts. Me again. It all fell back on me, again. Charlie's success or failure depended on my diligence, my patience. A warmth spread over my back just then, and I wondered what it might be. It was, of course, the glow emitted by the Wonder Family behind me. Their child would make it, surely. A Rhodes scholar, no doubt. Well, I determined, while their child was taking a break from counting his Nobel Prize money, he would not be munching on the donuts my son helped to bake!

Once Charlie overcame the initial traumas of going to school, riding the bus, and being with strangers, I began to allow myself some optimism. Charlie's education was beginning, and soon at least some of the problems we faced would be solved. Signing would come, followed shortly by speech and reading. Within a few months' time, we would be communicating on levels more nearly equal to his chronological and mental ages. I waited.

I continued to work with Charlie nearly every night and to reinforce what was reported to be happening at school. Once, feeling particularly proud of my efforts, I decided to tape one of our little sessions and to let his teacher critique my efforts. Naturally, I expected the highest praise, possibly an award of some kind. We were working with blocks of different shapes and colors that had to be put into the proper holes in a box. There on the tape were my sincere, if unrealistic, efforts to get Charlie to pay attention while I described shape and color. "Where is the red circle? Here it is. I have a red circle. Do you want a red circle? Here is the red circle. Where does the red circle go? Right!" The tape did not reveal that while I was making my descriptive chatter, Charlie was neither looking at me nor trying to put the block into the proper hole. He was trying to grab all the blocks away from me so he could leave the room. Anyway, his teacher tactfully told me that perhaps I should deal with one concept at a time. Name the object before working on color or shape. Taking her criticism in the constructive spirit in which it was offered, I put the blocks away and did not try that game again for many months.

The time passed slowly, weeks became months, and the difference in Charlie was imperceptible. Oh, he became accustomed to riding the bus and did begin to pay more attention when someone talked to him. He became a master imitator; he copied signs when they were directed at him. He did not, however, seem to understand nor to be interested in the connection between the signs he was copying and the objects they represented. Charlie imitated the sign for *water* when standing in front of the kitchen sink. "Do you want water?" I asked. Charlie signed back, "Water." (Aha, he wants some water.) When a glass of water was handed to him, Charlie looked completely baffled. "What is this for?" his face said, and he would try to give it back to me. School and sign classes notwithstanding, we still spent considerable time in the kitchen emptying the cabinets to find what Charlie wanted and fixing things for him that he did not eat.

My frustration returned and I began to wonder if I had done the right thing after all. Perhaps he had not been ready for school at age two. Perhaps it was not the right school. None of this, nor a whole host of other excuses rang true. I came right back to where I found myself almost constantly. I was not doing enough for Charlie. I had to work with him more. I had to stay with him, beside him, feeding him language every waking minute. The struggle between resentment for having to spend so much time with Charlie and the guilt for not spending nearly enough time with him raged within me. Whichever feeling won, I lost.

One Sunday afternoon when Charlie had been in school nearly a year and I had had quite my fill of fruitless attempts at being supermother, I sat selfishly watching television. Charlie was playing by himself; after all, children do have to develop their own resources for keeping themselves entertained. Besides, I couldn't go over "boy, baby, ball" one more time. I settled down to submerge my mind in some escapist entertainment when in walked Charlie. He walked over to my chair, and without a trace of hesitation, put three fingers (*w*) up to the corner of his mouth. "Water." This was the sign for water. It was one of those seemingly endless moments when one is not sure what is happening. My brain was trying to interpret what had just happened. Charlie had signed *water*. There was no water here. I had not signed water, so he was not imitating me.

The only alternative left was that he wanted some water and was here asking for it. By himself. Spontaneously. He had communicated with me, using language, for the first time in his life. He took my hand and led me to the kitchen, for I was still stunned by what had just happened. Once in front of the sink, my wits returned and I poured Charlie a glass of water. He drank it and asked for another. By now, my heart was pounding and my hands were shaking. I poured another glass, the water overflowing onto my trembling hand. I was laughing and crying at the same time, and I looked back at Charlie to make sure this was happening. I signed "water" again. I handed him the glass, but only let him have a sip. As I fell to my knees and threw my arms around him, the spilled water and my tears mixed together all over us both. He knew. At last, thank God, he knew. It would be weeks again before Charlie used a sign spontaneously, but this time the waiting was bearable.

5

People possess an abundance of wisdom, so much so that they feel compelled to share it. This is called advice. The problem is, that by taking advice, we admit that we are in some way inadequate for not coming up with their good idea ourselves. I think we are happiest about advice when it turns out not to be a good idea after all. One such piece of advice I received was that I should contact some other parents of a deaf child. This came to me from a friend about a year after I discovered Charlie's deafness. The logic was certainly sound. Other parents could offer a realistic picture of the tangle of negative feelings I was trapped in just then: guilt, hope, frustration, then more guilt. I felt guilty that I was not doing enough for Charlie. Then, he would pull me into hopefulness with some small success. I soared and redoubled my efforts, or at least promised to do so. Then, a snag or a missed response, a tantrum or a misunderstanding, and I plummeted downward again. I should have done more, more, more.

It seems that someone always knows someone (or someone who knows someone else) who is deaf. This time, my friend knew of a family with a deaf child who lived not far from my parents. After days of hesitation, I called.

"Hello, my name is Marcia Forecki. A mutual friend suggested that I call you. My son is deaf, and my friend mentioned that you have a little boy who is hearing impaired."

"Oh yes. She told me about you. I tried to call, but I didn't find your number in the book."

"Well, we live with my parents right now. I have a different name, even though I'm not married any more." (She doesn't want to hear about your divorce, you dope. And, don't you dare start crying.)

"How old is your little boy?"

"He's three."

"When did you find out?"

"When he was a year and a half. How old is your son? Five or six?"

"He's seven and in first grade."

"When did you find out about him?"

"Oh, he was about six months old." (My God! I wasted an entire year of Charlie's life.)

We chatted about this test and that doctor, the cost of hearing aids and therapists.

"Where does he go to school?" I asked.

"Well, right now he's in public school, and doing just beautifully. He's kept up with his classmates pretty well, though he is having some trouble with reading. We work with him every night, and it's coming along."

We talked for some time, ending with the mutual promise to meet soon and get the children together. It was to be several weeks before I called again. I realize now that my motivation for that second call was largely curiosity. I wanted to see what Charlie would be like in four years. I needed that hope. My friend had spoken so enthusiastically about how this little boy communicated with hearing people. He seemed to be the ideally adjusted child. "Obviously, his mother doesn't have to work," I thought. That old excuse of not being with Charlie during the day.

I bundled Charlie up for a crisp, late autumn ride. I told him with signs that we were going to meet a new friend. He was happy to be going for a ride, though he did not understand to where. Perhaps he had hopes of a new toy. His mind was such an enigma to me.

It was a particularly nasty day. I remember there was a bone-chilling drizzle, such as the Midwest conjures up to torture

69

me in particular. Charlie was delighted with the ride through suburban farms. When we pulled up into the strange driveway, he became uneasy. Gripping the seat belt, he refused to get out of the car. He was disappointed in our destination, but I tried to encourage him to come in with me. "A new friend," I kept telling him. "A communicating deaf child," I repeated to myself.

We were cordially greeted. The little boy I was so eager to hear stood before us. He wore a body aid, just like Charlie's. Charlie was instantly aware of the boy's hearing aid and seemed pleased to find someone else thus outfitted. After introductions were made among the adults, the boy's mother tapped his shoulder for attention. He peered into his mother's face as she explained that this was Charlie and Charlie's mother and could he say, "Hello, Charlie." I held my breath in anticipation. I understood not a word, although his mother praised his pretty speech. I was ready to leave.

Charlie stayed by me, even though the mother and the little boy tried to persuade him to go find some toys in the boy's room. We talked about programs in the area, and it became apparent that these people were oralists. I had contemplated the oral approach only briefly and discarded it. Language is more than speech, and my own need to communicate had me using gesture, pantomime, and fledgling signs even before I knew Charlie was deaf.

The boy's mother and I talked while the boys stared at each other. She told me about some of the community resources. The more she said, the more I realized that hers was a family that was truly coping. They were proud of their son's progress, and with reason. Were I to see him now, I'm sure I would be amazed. But then, expecting too much and hoping for more, I was devastated. After a time, the boy grew bored with playing with someone half his age and asked to watch television. This surprised but heartened me. The boy turned on the set and sat in front of a mute screen. The impression of those characters wandering silently across the screen, their actions disjointed and incomprehensible, was unforgettable. I began to fidget almost as obviously as Charlie. I searched for some excuse to leave.

70

We did not return to see these people, although I did have a few more phone conversations with them after our visit. At one point, the mother asked me not to sign to Charlie while we were at their house, as they did not allow their son to use any type of manual communication. We did not talk again after that. Had Charlie been confined to a wheelchair, would they have asked me to leave it at home so their son would continue to walk?

As we felt our way through those first months of deafness, little discoveries flew up at us. Not major enlightenments, but the little insights which ·leave one feeling rather stupid for not having seen them before.

I discovered the source of one of Charlie's behaviors one night at the dinner table. Meals are a major confrontation point for most mothers and their very young children. I was continually frustrated by Charlie's unwillingness to sit at the table for any period of time without fidgeting to get out of his chair. Even taking into account a child's natural aversion to anything resembling an organized adult activity—and with vegetables, yet—I felt that Charlie's restlessness was excessive. After repeatedly scolding him to sit still, I realized what the problem was. Our phone invariably rang during dinner. Charlie didn't know this, but what he did know was that at some point in the meal, one of the adults usually jumped up, left for a while, and then came back. He was merely taking his rightful turn at this.

The next time the phone rang, I told Charlie what was happening and took him in with me to answer it. After that, whenever the phone would ring, I simply announced to Charlie that Grandpa or I was leaving the table or the room to answer the phone. He was then perfectly content to stay put, confident that whoever went to answer the phone would be back. The mystery was solved.

It took me a while to understand Charlie's reaction to being teased. Teasing is usually a favorite game for toddlers, but it was not so for Charlie. Tickling and peek-a-boo were obvious enough that they did not baffle him. But, the practice of taking a toy and saying, "Mine," or "I'm going to get you," and various other torments perpetrated by adults did not amuse Charlie. I saw the hurt or sometimes fearful look on his face when we came after him, all in good fun. Then, by some blast of insight, I understood that he was unable to catch the nuance of voice that usually gave away a tease. A mean face on a person saying, "I'm going to catch you and hug you and kiss you," was just a mean face to Charlie. We had to let our facial expressions reveal the joke, such as a mean face followed immediately by some exaggerated silliness. Once onto this, Charlie became not only the willing victim but the enthusiastic tormentor.

The second summer after Charlie began preschool, we attended a week-long meeting for parents and childen at our state school for the deaf. I had to give up one week of my vacation, but never mind, any sacrifice for the cause. These meetings, called family learning vacations, are designed primarily for the benefit of the parents. There are plenty of activities for the deaf children and their siblings so that their parents can attend the various lectures and discussions throughout the day.

At the meeting we attended, the various sessions were led by educators, deaf adults, and social service people. The days were long and the discussion sessions among the parents ran late into the night. Families stayed together in the dormitories, so educationally and family-living wise, it was an intense week.

I went to the meeting with high expectations, and many of them were met. However, it wasn't long before I was raising my defenses. I felt that going to a meeting such as this was an admission that I had a problem. Let's face it, most families do not spend their vacations housed together in a children's dormitory where they have to share the bathroom with strangers and stoop under the shower.

The first night in our make-shift lounge, where the parents congregated after the children were put to bed, was the time for feeling one another out. Actually, we seemed to be trying to affirm our own behavior as parents as we compared it to what other parents had done. When did you discover your child's deafness? was a critical question. If the other parent had discovered his or her child's deafness before I had, it implied that I had been less sensitive than he or she. I never answered that question until the other parent did, so that I could give one of two responses. If I had discovered earlier, then I could be generous and admit that it was difficult to detect and that my parents had been a great help. If I had been later, then I explained how becoming a single parent had somewhat preoccupied me and kept me from getting anything done, although, of course, I had suspected it. I was so afraid of being thought ill of by these people, many of whom seemed to be coping better than I. These, then, were my and Charlie's competition.

Another question during comparison period was, Do you sign? Some parents were just beginning to sign. Some had tried an oral approach for a while before giving into the need for immediate communication.

At one of our nightly rehashes, we discussed our conversations with the deaf adults at this meeting. Some of these teachers and business people had started their education in oral programs. It was their choice, later, to learn sign language because they felt the need to communicate with other deaf people. Meeting these people was the most exciting and uplifting experience for me since I had started this whole business. These working, functioning adults proved that the notion of sign language holding deaf people down is absurd. Maybe Charlie could grow up, after all. Maybe he would make it to independent adulthood.

I went through a small metamorphosis during the week at the family learning vacation. At first, coming in a stranger and feeling less than confident of myself as a coping parent, the leaders of the meeting (the professionals) seemed very important, and I looked to them with admiration. They knew what to do and I did not. As the days passed and the parents became closer to each other, my own confidence grew. I was not the only parent facing the problems of living with and educating a deaf child. Here were other parents dealing with the same problems I faced. I began to learn from their successes and to offer advice from mine. The parents began to form a unit and, as we did so, the professionals began to look different to me. They became outsiders. Oh sure, they had formal education and experience in dealing with this problem, but for them it was a job. They left it at night and went home to a normal family where people talked at dinner without having to tap the table or lay down their forks. They could read their children a story at bedtime, or they had no children and could do whatever they liked. I became skeptical of their advice on living outside of the classroom. The other parents and the deaf adults had become my allies; the rest didn't know what I dealt with.

One evening, when the children were asleep and the parents had abandoned the lounge, I couldn't sleep. I needed time to digest the blitzkreig of information, ideas, and perceptions I had been receiving each day, time to make them a part of my own understanding. I had picked up several pamphlets from a display in one of the sign language classrooms. I started, absently at first, to thumb through them. One told about captioned television, another listed career opportunities for the deaf, and another concerned methods of dealing with deaf children. Not much new here. The same kind of hopeful good news on how far we have come and how open the future is for the next generation of deaf adults.

There was plain talk here, too: underemployment as a continuing problem for the deaf, the slow progress of young children deaf from birth, and the staggering statistic that nearly 95 percent of profoundly deaf people choose deaf spouses. Nearly all. It seemed natural enough, but, as I thought more, I realized that this was more than demographics on who marries whom. My son would likely choose a deaf wife from among his deaf friends. Where would this put me? What about the rest of the family? How would Charlie's wife view me? She would be able to share a part of him that was closed to me. There are parts of Charlie I do not understand and can never understand. No matter how hard I work.

Toward the end of our week at the school for the deaf, when the parents had become acquainted and felt comfortable opening up, a serious discussion was scheduled for the parents; the fathers in one room and the mothers in another. It was apparently believed that the parental roles were different, and the discussions should be separate. Being the only single parent there, I wondered which discussion I ought to attend. Maybe I could run back and forth between them!

The professionals delved and the mothers in my room obediently responded to their probing and rather personal questions. I remained silent. I would have said nothing at all, despite the professionals' efforts to draw me out, had not one of the more capable mothers made the statement that her family had had problems at first but now they felt they had adjusted and were coping quite well. I could not keep still, especially not when several others added their confirmation that they felt the same way. At the risk of showing my weakness, I pointed out that it was not possible for me to say I had fully accepted Charlie's deafness when new ramifications kept manifesting themselves. Each new problem brought new doubts, the need for more information, and renewed determination to work harder to deal with Charlie's new problem. I did not know what difficulties lay in Charlie's future growth and development, but I was certainly not prepared to say that I had coped with Charlie's deafness successfully. There was still room for failure.

Leaving the discussion, I went off to bed, the hour being late. I knew that in the morning everyone would be looking for me, the parent who, by her own admission, had not yet fully coped. I was spared that ordeal, however. When I awoke the next day, Charlie was ill. In fact, we left the meeting a day early. Charlie developed pneumonia after we returned home. So, having spent one of my vacation weeks at the parents' meeting, I proceeded to spend the second week at home with a pneumonia-stricken child. A true mother's holiday.

As Charlie approached four, I knew it was time to reassess. After two pitifully slow years, we were beginning to see some progress. In most ways, Charlie behaved like any four-year-old. He had control of his body. He could ride a tricycle, run, jump, and go to the bathroom when sufficiently nagged. He was gaining some control over his environment. He knew the general household routine. He understood when I told him it was mealtime or bathtime. He also understood bedtime but feigned confusion with an excessively blank look. Charlie was gaining some control over other people. He could ask for what he wanted. He had learned that an attempt at speaking, however halfhearted, could get him nearly anything. He had absolute control over me. I went to him when he called "Ba" (my name for a very long time). He could turn his enormous hazel eyes imploringly in my direction with great success.

But, as I looked critically at Charlie, I knew it was time to make some more decisions. He had come so far, and yet, his language consisted of single-word signs. He had a good number of nouns, but few verbs. He could only speak about things he could see. He could not talk about the past or the future. He did not know his name, nor mine, apart from the name signs. He could not speak intelligibly except for a few words such as *more* and *no*. He did not understand organized games. It seemed the older he became the more obvious were his deficiencies. Clearly, it was time for me to take action. In the quest for a place in the parenthood Hall of Fame, one must keep moving forward. If you stop too long, you begin to roll backwards.

Despite Charlie's illness after we returned home from the family learning vacation at our state school for the deaf, it was very clear to me that Charlie not only could handle being in school all day, but that he desperately needed it. A few hours a week in preschool, as good as it was, simply was not enough.

The decision to place Charlie in a school for the deaf was like the decision to use sign language. It made itself for me. I had seen the kinds of learning a state school offered. It was hardly the bars-on-the-window, uniform-wearing, straight-lines-of-silent-children place of another, more ignorant time. The schools were staffed with professional, caring teachers and counselors. The students came first in these schools. With a teacher/student ratio of one teacher for each four or five students, state schools were ahead of public school instruction in personal attention. Besides, public school was beyond Charlie, at least then. He would have been swallowed up in a classroom of thirty children with a teacher who did not know sign language, an interpreter who was with him only part of the day, and students who could not truly be considered his peers academically or socially. This meant there was but one place in most states where Charlie could receive a free public education. (The key word here is *free*.) I began to inquire and found that not all state schools had a preschool program. Since the law does not require free education for handicapped children before the age of five, some states provided a preschool and others did not.

I made a list of schools to visit. Starting with the state schools located in forty-eight states, I eliminated the schools that did not have a preschool program. Charlie was still a year and a half away from kindergarten. Schools located in very small towns where job opportunities would be limited for me were crossed off the list. I also crossed out schools more than a few hundred miles from my family. I was left with one school—the Iowa School for the Deaf. One school in the entire continental United States. One school in the Western Hemisphere. There was but one place in the solar system where my son could go to school. Because of Charlie, I had to narrow my universe to one town where he could go to school. With that background, it is not at all difficult to see that I considered moving to be absolutely the most selfless sacrifice any mother had ever been called upon to make. I would be giving up a job, friends, and the support and comfort of my family for Charlie. I would toss aside my future, which suddenly seemed as bright as a nova (after all, I was giving it up). This would surely put me in the running for a Nobel prize, if not sainthood. (I preferred the Nobel prize, actually, since sainthood seemed to require one to die, and there was no cash award of which I was aware.)

Before committing myself irrevocably to the move to Iowa, I would have to visit the school for the deaf. I was down about the trip and about the move. I was delightfully down. As every mother knows, there is nothing quite like the self-satisfaction that comes from wallowing in the pit of martyrdom. An additional joy would come from the admiration I would surely receive for my self-denial.

Before I made plans to visit the school, I talked about my difficult decision to my friends. Why not give them a last chance to admire me before I left.

"I just don't know what I'm going to do with Charlie," I began one day during a coffee break at work, eyes appropriately downcast. I knew perfectly well what I was going to do—find the best school I could and take Charlie there. Decisions are so much easier when one has no choice at all.

"Is something wrong?" someone asked.

"Well, nothing new. It's just that Charlie is nearly four, and I think he needs to be in school every day."

"But, he's so young."

"I know that. But, he has so far to go. Each minute he is not learning puts him farther back." (Sigh here, indicating fatigue.)

"Isn't there another preschool you could put him in?"

"Nothing." I had the attention of most of the table, now. Friends are great. They follow the script so well.

"Have you talked to the school board?"

"Yes. I've called. There is a kindergarten for hearing-impaired children. But, Charlie won't be eligible for another year and a half. He's so ready to learn now. I just can't waste that time. I'll have to see about one of the state schools for the deaf."

I thought I heard a gasp from my audience. Probably only the coffee maker cleaning itself.

"Do you think that's wise?" asked a new employee. Unlike the others, she had not been with me since the discovery of Charlie's deafness. Poor thing. Why didn't someone warn her of the tirade she was inviting. "If she says *mainstream*, I think I'll let her have it," I thought.

"The public schools have lots of programs for the handicapped, now. My Terri has a boy in her class in a wheelchair. All the kids think it's neat. I think it's good for everyone. The handicapped child doesn't get left out, and the other children learn to be tolerant of people who are different."

"Being in a wheelchair is nothing like being profoundly deaf. The situations are not comparable." I noticed my friends sit back somewhat in their chairs. "From a wheelchair, a child can still communicate, can know what the teacher is saying, and can know what classmates are saying. They all speak the same language. How many classroom teachers have you met who know sign language?"

"What about interpreters?"

"Yes. An interpreter will tell Charlie what the teacher says. But, not what the kid behind him says. When the others are laughing, will the interpreter explain the joke? Will the interpreter go with him to the lunchroom? To the playground? To the gym? To the bathroom?"

My friends were talking among themselves now. The new employee was beginning to glance around the table, looking for an opportunity to jump into someone else's conversation. Unable to do so, or perhaps just a bit masochistic, she said, "But, don't you think it's important for Charlie to learn to live in a hearing world?"

Now the scrape of chairs skidding back from the table. There were still five minutes of the break left, but I guess even the prospect of returning to work held more appeal than listening to my oft-repeated answer to this one.

"Charlie has lived in a hearing world all his life. He always will live in a hearing world. How can he not learn to live in it? He does live in it. What he needs to learn is about himself, how and why he is different. That there are other children like himself. That he has peers, equals. He needs to know deaf adults. He needs to see that deaf people grow up, have jobs, raise families. He can't get that in public school. He can't get self-esteem except from people like himself." (I should have added, "I think." How did I know if this was true? But, it would have diminished my impact. Besides, I believed it was true. I still do. I think.)

Everyone had by now left the room. Poor woman. She returned to her desk humbled and late. I felt stupid, once again.

There was really no need to attack someone for asking a reasonable question. Who was I to be so pompous? Until Charlie came along I held essentially the same opinions as this woman. Throw all children together, mix well, and you'll turn out tolerance. It sounded logical enough. Maybe it would even work.

As I recall, the unfortunate woman who had been so ill-advised as to question the mother of a handicapped child left her job within a short time. I remember distinctly that she did not sit at my table for coffee after that fateful day. I think she took up crochet or something. No doubt to settle her nerves.

The trip to visit the school for the deaf in Iowa was exciting. In the first place, it was a big secret (except from a select multitude of my friends). Until my plans were set I thought it best not to let my employer know I was contemplating leaving. The trip was an adventure. I was doing something really important for Charlie. I had fantasies about the image I would project to the school staff. Here I was, a woman willing to put her own opportunity aside for her child. It was very much the same feeling that I had when I first visited Charlie's preschool. I would knock them dead with my expertise, my strength, my sacrifice. This time, I really would. Besides, none of these people knew anything about me, so I had a good chance to pull it off.

I didn't take Charlie with me on that first visit for several reasons. I wanted a few days away from him. I also wanted to be able to look around objectively. If Charlie reacted badly to the facilities or the people, whether from shyness or fatigue or general stubbornness, it could affect my decision. I was now deciding for both of us where we would live, where I would work, who we would know—the whole direction of two lives. It had to be right. If Charlie were a hearing child, I could live anywhere I wanted and could send him to the school down the street. But he wasn't, and I couldn't.

Driving onto the grounds of the school, I noticed a track meet was in progress. The school bus parked off to the side indicated that this was a meet with another school. "Great," I thought. "Competition with other schools. Remember to ask if they play against public schools." I pulled my car over and parked by the side of the road to watch the runners take their marks for a hurdles race. I noticed all the hurdles seemed to be standard height. No shorter for deaf runners. The boys got down in their set positions and looked up. Standing by the line was an official with . . . it couldn't be . . . it was . . . a pistol!

"He is not going to start this race with a gun. Unfair. Foul," I shouted in my mind. I put my hand on the car door, prepared to get out and stop the race.

"Wait. Stop the race." I saw myself marching up to the official, hands on hips. *"What do you mean starting this race with a gun. These boys and girls are deaf. Who put you in charge of this race, anyway? What's your name?"*

"Ma'am, would you please get off the track. We're about to start a race here."

"Race! This is a mockery." I pictured the runners all leaving their marks. They were walking toward us, their faces wearing puzzled looks. They signed questions to each other as they came closer. *"You see?"* I turned back to the official, *"They want to know what is going on here."*

"Ma'am, who are you?"

"Who am I? Why, I am a MOTHER." I turned to the boys and girls who were encircling us now. *"Mother,"* I signed, pointing to myself.

When the deaf children were close enough for me to read their signs and to see their faces, I could see they were not so much puzzled as annoyed. What was that sign they were giving me? Go away! But, I am trying to help. I turned back to the official, who was now wearing a very smug expression. *"Would you mind picking up the hurdles you knocked over, Ma'am."*

My fantasy was shattered by the crack of a gunshot. Instantly, the runners were off. All of them at once. Truly this school could work miracles.

After a brief introduction at the superintendent's office, I met John, the guide who was to show me around the school. I was a little disappointed in myself for being relieved that he could hear. As we began walking toward our first destination, I asked about the track meet.

"Our team has done real well this year."

"Do they play only schools for the deaf?" I asked.

"Oh no. The school they are playing today is a public school from the town just down the highway. We play some deaf schools and some hearing schools."

"Well, I noticed that they started the race with a gun."

"Actually, it's a starter's pistol. Fires blanks. Perfectly harmless."

"Yes, but can the kids . . . I mean . . . you know."

"Can our kids hear it?" I'm sure my guide was convinced that he had one of *those* mothers and would be tied up answering stupid questions all afternoon. I thought I heard just the beginning of a disgusted sigh, but maybe not. "Some of the kids can hear the starter's pistol. The rest watch for the smoke."

Would that give the hearing kids the advantage over the deaf? I was trying to remember if sound traveled faster than light or vice versa. It seemed like Einstein belonged here somewhere, but I couldn't quite make him fit.

I saw everything at the school: classrooms in session, resource rooms, labs, dorms, the pool, the infirmary, the vocational center. Each new sight impressed me more than the last.

The cafeteria was a bit of a shock. Usually there is such a din in a school lunchroom that one can barely think. Here it was quiet. Except for an occasional yell from a little one, the main noise was the scraping of stainless steel on plastic plates and the thud of plastic glasses on plastic trays. I wondered why such places make one want to whisper.

I noticed as John led me around campus that the students walking along together were not talking to each other. They were signing faster than I could follow. Each time we passed a student, John would tell me his or her name, what town he or she came from and, inevitably, some little distinguishing tidbit. (I wondered what Charlie's little distinction might be, later, for others on tour. "That's Charlie. His mother quit her job to bring him here to school. She still signs like she has mittens on, though.") John knew all of these kids.

"Hey, Dwight. Did you bring that new bike seat from home last weekend?"

"Yes. It's in my room."

"I'll help you put it on later."

So they could talk. The kids only signed to each other, but as John spoke and signed to the older kids, they signed and spoke back. Some of these kids had phenomenal speech. I was amazed.

"Some of these kids speak so well."

"Oh sure. Some have more hearing than others, of course. But most all do pretty well."

"But, they don't seem to talk much to each other." I always have to take it one step too far.

"Not much point, really, in that, is there?"

For the first time, I had a very intense feeling of being an outsider. I was different from all of these kids and many of the staff members. I was in deaf territory. The kids looked so at ease with each other. Did they feel as comfortable here as they looked? Had I done something right in choosing this school, after all?

While I was marveling at the rapid signing among the students and the teachers and staff, I began to lose track of who was deaf and who was hearing. I found myself looking for a hearing aid every time I was introduced to an adult. (With the kids, at least, I could be sure.) I met one teacher and signed, "Hello." My guide introduced me, and he was signing. All right. She is deaf.

"My son will start school here soon," I said, proud that I had made it through an entire sentence without knocking my hands together. The teacher obviously could tell that I was hearing, for she answered verbally, "That's great. Is he with you, now?"

"He is at home in . . ." I started to spell Kansas City and confused *a* with *s* . My hands dropped to my side and I chattered like someone released from a vow of silence, relieved that I did not have to embarrass myself further. I knew that my signs were all right for a child, but with adults I frequently got tangled up with my spelling. Trying to read someone else's spelling is even worse than doing it one's self. Reading the fingerspelling of a deaf adult at normal speed is like trying to count drops of water in the shower. At least this time I was saved.

I did not, however, make it through the afternoon unscathed. John left me in the teacher's lounge with a cup of coffee while he made a phone call. A young man came in and sat down at the table with me. I must have been looking at him, probably searching for a hearing aid. He signed and said, "Hello." From his voice, I could tell that he was deaf. I smiled and looked at my cup. When I had seen everything that could possibly be observed about a cup of coffee, I timidly looked up. We exchanged smiles again. His was confident and cheerful. Mine felt like the smile one gets from a sour grapefruit. It probably looked worse.

"Are you a parent?" he asked.

"Yes. My son will start school here soon," I answered. (I had that down pretty well after repeating it all day.)

"Are you deaf?" he asked.

"Yes," I answered. (Somehow, I thought we were still talking about Charlie.)

"Did you go to school here?"

"Yes." (I caught the signs *school here*. Yes, I explained that before. I still thought we were talking about Charlie.)

"Did you graduate?" (I read the sign *grade*.)

"Kindergarten."

He gave me a rather surprised look and then went back to reading his book. Why did he end the conversation just when I was starting to roll, I wondered. Probably to prepare for his next class.

John opened the door just then and I turned around. "Just be another minute," he said.

"No problem," I answered. I turned back around to find the young teacher smiling at me. It was a rather different smile than he had worn before. He gathered up his books, waved good-bye, and left.

I sat contentedly going over our little conversation. I had done rather well, I thought. I'll bet not every parent can just pick up a sign conversation like that. I wanted to remember the signs. "Parent." "You deaf?" What? In the slow motion instant replay in my mind I saw the signs clearly. "Are you deaf?" I had said yes. He said did *I* go to school here, not Charlie. *G* curving up from the hand; that's *graduate*. Did you graduate? Oh my God. Instead of telling him my deaf son would be starting kindergarten here, I said I had graduated from kindergarten here. I sank to the floor and melted through. I thought I was reading him so well. That's it. I can't bring Charlie to school here. By the time I get him here the whole school will know what I said. I heard laughter as the students passed in the hall between classes. They had heard about it already. Charlie didn't have a chance here, now. But then, he had even less of a chance with me at home. When John came back, I told him I had seen enough. "I love the school. When can Charlie begin?" I asked, trying to hide the urgency I suddenly felt.

"He can start the day he moves to town."

"Great." Maybe if I got Charlie here fast enough the news will not have spread too far about me.

We were nearly finished with our tour anyway. I had asked all the questions I could think of but still elicited a promise that I could call or write if I thought of something else. John took me back to the elementary building so I could chat with the principal about the paper procedures for enrolling Charlie. I thanked John for his great help and waited in the hall while the principal finished up a phone call.

The hall was brightly decorated with circus posters and scenes. Apparently, there had been a trip to the circus because the children had drawn pictures of clowns and elephants, which were also hanging in the hall.

There was a little boy coming down the hall just then, probably on his way back from speech class or the restroom. I smiled at him. I thought that maybe I could say something to him without repeating my humiliating performance in the teacher's lounge. He was just a kid, about Charlie's age. Just to be safe, I kept it simple.

"Hi," I signed.

"Hi," he responded. My confidence rose.

"Did you go to the circus?" I asked. He looked puzzled. "Circus," I repeated. Still the blank stare. (The one Charlie is so good at.) I pointed to the picture on the wall beside him. "Did you go to the circus?"

He lifted his head in annoyed understanding, then took my right hand in his and slapped it lightly. Before I could pull it back, he turned my right hand over and guided me in repeating the sign for *circus*, correctly this time. "Yes," he signed. "Thanks," I said and let him go. I was saved by the principal coming out to fetch me and to shoo this smart-handed student back to class. "Corrected by a child," I thought as I followed the principal into her office. "And these are the *unfortunate* ones?"

Without describing the quality of the facilities, the dedication of the staff, or the care with which the children were treated as individuals, I will only say that I found what I believed to be the best possible school for Charlie. That decision is probably the only one I have been absolutely sure of in my entire life. Now, with the easy part behind, I had to deal with getting Charlie to his new school. Fall was approaching. I didn't want to move in a blizzard, so I decided to wait until after the holidays. We would move after the first of the year.

Quitting my job was a bit frightening. I knew I would best be able to find work in the new town after I was actually there. So, I resigned. For a short time I felt the rush of excitement. Everyone wished me well. I was congratulated, admired, and assured that I was doing the right thing.

This wasn't the first time I had left home. I had gone off to college, then off to be married. When each had ended, I came home. Just as with the other departures, I felt good and bad about leaving. I would miss the companionship, but I longed for the freedom. I think I wanted Charlie to have me for his parent; only me.

Mom must have sensed that I needed her less and less. We agreed even more rarely now. She never came right out and said, "Don't go." She never would have done that. But, she did find ways to show that she was not ready for us to leave. For instance, she feared aloud that the family would lose its ability to communicate with Charlie.

"You'll both be so far away. I know what you are doing is the best . . ."

"It is the *only* . . ."

"Yes, probably the only thing for Charlie."

"We'll only be two hundred miles away, Mom. We'll be back often. Maybe more often than you would like," I said with a forced laugh. My laughter was not returned. "You won't forget your signs. Don't worry."

"But, Charlie will be learning new signs all the time. How will we keep up?"

"He'll also be learning to talk and to speechread, you know," I sounded reassuring, even comforting.

There was a switch: me being the optimistic one, and Mother sounding fearful. But, don't be deceived. Whatever confidence I may have felt was in the school, not in myself. I was too pleased with my decision to be really worried about the move.

"I'll find a job soon and we'll both be on our way," I kept telling everyone, loud enough that I could hear, too.

My mother's fears turned out to be for naught. The family has not lost its ability to communicate with Charlie. They have all made great efforts to keep up. My father, who had not been in a classroom for longer than he would let me tell you, enrolled in a sign class. I think I love him more for that than for anything else, ever.

6

The winter of 1980–81 was one of the mildest midwesterners had seen in decades. In this part of the country, the month of January can produce enough nastiness to make one stay home from the after-Christmas sales. (Why do you think they call them *white sales*?) But, this particular year, January dropped only the lightest dusting of snow and temperatures remained well above the cabin-fever level. Perhaps the mild weather and the false confidence it fostered were factors in my decision to move Charlie into his new school in the middle of the term.

The move was scheduled for February 1. That morning the temperatures began to drop. With them dropped snow, lightly, but unceasingly, all day. By the time the truck, driven by my friend Allen, and my car were packed, winter storm warnings were out. Before we reached the corner, the term being used by those irritatingly pleasant weather forecasters on the radio was *blizzard*. Should we go on and try to outrun the snow or wait? I hadn't really left home yet, and already my new life was throwing decisions at me.

Since Charlie wasn't going up on the initial trip but was remaining behind a week or so with my parents, the only ones in jeopardy were two adults. I knew I was crazy enough to go. My friend was crazy enough to leave the decision to a madwoman, so he deserved what he got.

At first it was a benign snow. Visibility was good, the roads clear. "Four hours. That's all I ask," I spoke softly to the forces of nature from inside my car. "Just let us get there and unpack the vehicles, and I promise I will never curse snow again. Perhaps an occasional word of constructive criticism."

It became obvious that no one heard me. After only two hours we began to move at a crawl. I could make out only the red lights of my friend's pickup ahead of me and the line dividing the highway from the shoulder. I wondered if he had that much guidance. The thought of dutifully following those little red beacons into the ditch flitted through my mind. Constantly. Worse yet, what if those lights didn't belong to his truck? Faith, dear girl, faith. Anyone on as noble a journey as this would surely be looked after.

I had traveled this road once before when I came up to find an apartment. But, now, all I could see in every direction was swirling white. Road signs or markers were only visible for the instant just before I passed them. "Wait until they hear about this," I thought. "Everyone will be impressed at the determination this has taken." I could tell by my odometer, now the only reliable point of reference, that we were nearly there. Relaxing just a bit, I realized how stiff my neck and shoulders were from gripping the steering wheel against the gale winds and from straining to see anything ahead of me. The two little red lights seemed like pinpoints now. A trip that should have taken four hours had now taken over six.

Then, something went wrong. The car began to slow. I looked down at the speedometer needle and watched it fall steadily backward. I looked up again. The two red lights were gone. My car had nearly come to a stop. If I didn't get over, I would surely be rammed by whoever was behind me. If I overshot the shoulder, I could become stuck in the ditch, or worse.

I turned the wheel and eased my way off the road just as my car came to a full stop. I tried the engine and it started. I tried easing the clutch out ever so gently while grazing the accelerator with my right foot. I moved slowly forward. Now, second gear. Easy. Gears engaged. The car died. After several more tries, I found that I was only able to inch forward a few feet before the engine ceased running.

All my common-sense emergency advice came back to me. (Stay in the car. Turn on the flashers. Turn the engine on occasionally for heat. Don't panic. Wait for help.) With all the clothes that were packed in the car, I knew I would not freeze. "If you have to go to the bathroom, now," I threatened myself, "I'll hate you forever." I bundled up as best I could. "What is wrong with the car? Think. Probably just some little thing you're doing wrong. Try again. Think." I tried moving forward again. As before, the car died whenever it was moving faster than about three miles per hour. What could be wrong with a six-month-old car? Japanese, yet! Where is the answer man when you need him?

It was after the first hour that I became aware that my feet were getting numb. I huddled under a pile of clothes, trying to draw my feet up under my body. Not easy in a bucket seat, even for someone of my diminutive size. I also became aware about then that there were very few cars out on the highway. As night approached, there would be even fewer. Those that did pass probably could not even see me until they were parallel to me. The wind was now blowing the snow very hard in every direction at once. I nearly lost my bearings. Left freeway, right cornfield. Both sides looked identical in the snow.

Panic had been circling about and now settled in on me. What if I died here by the side of this road? I would be a failure. What would become of Charlie? Who would take care of him? Would he remember me and why I died? For him. Always for him.

> *"Where is your mother, little boy?"*
> *"She died."*
> *"Oh, I'm so sorry. What happened?"*
> *"She tried to move north in February in a blizzard. Even lost our TV."*
> *"You poor thing. Well, probably for the best."*

I was hallucinating. It was cold, colder than I ever remember it being before or since. I ran the engine for a very few minutes at a time, trying to conserve fuel. It now seemed probable that I would be out here all night. My flat half-can of diet soda would have to last me who knows how long. Well, maybe if I pulled through this, I could do a commercial: "I survived three days on six ounces of plain label diet orange." Charlie could brag about that to his little friends.

A car went by and I saw the brake lights go on. It went a little further up the road and turned across the median. I turned around as best I could, cramped under my pile of clothes. (Is this what it would be like to fall in a Goodwill bin?) The car was coming back across the median. It stopped. I waited while a little, huddled person fought the wind to my door. "What if he is a psychotic killer? Don't open the door," I thought. Then, "You idiot, even a murderer would be in a warm house in this storm. Someone's warm house." I rolled down the window a crack. A blast of snow blew in on me.

"You got trouble, lady?"

"My car just quit on me."

"You'll freeze out here. Let me give you a lift into town," he shouted above the wind.

"I was following someone," I shouted back. "He'll be back soon, I'm sure."

"It's 40° below out here, lady."

"But, if he comes back and I'm gone . . ."

"Suit yourself."

"Thank you anyway," I shouted to his back. The stranger trudged off, got in his car, and pulled away. I thought afterward I should have asked if he had something to eat.

"Allen will be back for me," I reassured myself. "As soon as he sees I'm not behind him, he'll turn around." I pulled off one mitten and looked at my watch. I had been here over an hour. The town couldn't be that far ahead. Where was he?

"Allen," I said aloud, "come back for me." Hearing the fear in my own voice was terrifying. "Allen," I shouted, "come get me."

I screamed until my throat hurt and then I cried. Between wind gusts, I had seen a farm house off to the right, back from the road a good distance. Maybe I could go there. If Allen came and found the car empty. . . . I could leave a note. I strained to see the farm house through the snow. Where were the lights? Wasn't anybody home? They must be home. Where is there to go around here? Maybe the power went off. Of course, the lights went out in the storm. Could I get to the house? I was afraid I couldn't. I remembered hearing about a woman who wandered around in a blizzard; she became lost and died only a few feet from a house. No, if I was to die I would do it in my own car. It wasn't paid for, but then that would be the bank's problem, not mine. They couldn't come back at Charlie, could they? No. I was sure the debt ended with my death. "Sort of like taking it with me," I laughed. My laughter sounded shrill and hysterical. "Allen," I began to scream again.

Each time I saw headlights in my rearview mirror, I rolled down the window. "Stop. Help me." I screamed. The cars passed very infrequently.

I saw headlights in the opposite lane, coming toward me. They were higher than a car's lights. A pickup, maybe? It was going very slowly. I rolled down the window and squinted against the flying snow. The other car's window was down, too. "Allen," I called. He couldn't possibly have heard. I waved frantically out the window. The truck turned on the median, pulled up behind me and stopped. Allen got out and ran toward me. I tried to throw off the pile of clothes and get out, but I was too stiff to move. I was also suddenly very aware that I needed to go to the bathroom.

Allen asked me what was wrong with my car. I was crying by now and had trouble explaining. He wanted to try the engine. I got out and stood by the side of the road. (My television was in the passenger seat, so there was only room for one person to sit in the car.) Allen determined that there was frozen water in the gas line. He produced a bottle of something and poured it into my gas tank. "Now try," he said. Grateful to get back into the car and out of the wind, I tried it. First gear. Second gear. Third gear. The car felt and sounded like the first day I bought it. I flashed my lights to signal that all was well, and turned back onto the highway. As I shifted confidently into fourth gear, I saw a road sign. I had been sitting fifteen miles from town. I was too glad to be alive to wonder why it had taken Allen over two hours to find me along fifteen miles of highway. But, I did mention it later, several times.

That first week in the apartment was great fun. The blizzard had ended the night I arrived and by the next day, things were warming up. It is ever thus for me.

As I checked each item off my list of things to get done before Charlie arrived, I felt exhilarated. This is how success must feel, I thought. In only a few days' time, my plans of the last several months would be fulfilled. A new home, a new (read better) job, and Charlie in a good school. I smiled to myself a lot that week.

I spent a good deal of time and money making Charlie's new room inviting for him. I had brought some of his toys when I came up initially so they would be waiting for him. I sewed colorful curtains and hung cheery posters. I bought Charlie a captain's bed and put it together myself. The first time, I got the drawers in upside down, but not discouraged, I threw the instructions away and started over. When I carried the huge pieces of packing cardboard out to the dumpster, the wind caught them like sails and I fell backwards several times. But, I didn't mind. I rather suspect my neighbors enjoyed watching, but the prospect of their laughter behind bedsheet draperies failed to sink my spirits.

Everything about this move felt absolutely right. I was enjoying my freedom and my competence. Next week, with Charlie securely tucked in at school, I would begin an earnest job search. Then, I could begin spending some of my savings to replace the borrowed furnishings I had set up so carefully (and sparsely) in my apartment. My mind was racing weeks and months ahead to all the things Charlie and I would do together. Nothing could get me down now, I believed.

When I brought Charlie to his new home, I tried to prepare him all the way. "We are going to live in a new house." (I didn't know the sign for apartment, but Charlie didn't know it either.) "Charlie is going to a new school." He nodded in indifferent agreement. This was our first long auto trip together. The first

93

of many between our house and Grandpa and Grandma's house. The car was loaded with Charlie's clothes and toys. He knew this was no ordinary outing, and his demeanor reflected his apprehension.

When we finally reached our new home, I ushered Charlie in with a flourish, half expecting him to say it was great, or something. Instead, he stood just inside the door as if waiting for someone to come and greet us. Why not? I took him down the short hall to his room and told him, "This is Charlie's room." He stood on his toes and leaned into the room. He craned his neck so that only as much of his head as was needed to look around was actually in the room. When he recognized some of his things, he looked at me with a puzzled expression. "This is your own room," I told him proudly. "See," I continued the tour, "your bed, your books, Charlie's toys, Charlie's clothes, Charlie's shoes." He remained in his position, straddling the threshold diplomatically, and watched me go from item to item. He was quite unimpressed.

Charlie helped me unload the car, move his things in, and put them away. I kept up an excited chatter, whenever my hands were free. I hoped my excitement would be contagious. Charlie walked slowly from room to room, a solemn expression on his face. He was resigning himself to this place. While I was hanging Charlie's clothes in his new closet, he tapped me on the leg. I turned around with a smile. Charlie had his coat and hat on. He signed, "Home." Enough of this adventure, he was ready to go home.

Charlie's pose of temporarily accepting things until we could return home extended to his new school. I took him the first day, fairly beaming with pride. Here was the boy they had probably been so concerned about since my first visit. The principal of the elementary school and I showed Charlie around the building. I'm sure he thought that the rooms and the pictures were interesting enough, but he made no attempt to show it. I shall have to wait until Charlie grows up to find out if he realized that first day that this would be his school every day.

Charlie's new teacher and her aide patiently showed Charlie his new classroom and introduced him to his classmates. Charlie's name was already on the bulletin board and there was a place for him at the table. The teacher pried Charlie away from me long enough to take a picture of him. It later came home in his valentine to me. I still have it. I have entitled it *Abandonment*.

I left Charlie in his classroom screaming piteously. I only got a few feet down the hall when I stopped. The tears that had been welling up since I woke up that morning had finally overflowed. I dug unceremoniously in my purse for a tissue. While I took care of myself, I noted a change in the hallway. Something was different. There was no sound of wailing following me down the hall. Charlie had stopped crying. This was great. Yes, he would be fine soon. When he got used to everything. I wondered with what activity the teacher had captured Charlie's attention. Maybe if I could just steal back quietly. I wouldn't go in the door. I would just take a quick peek. As I passed the classroom door, I saw the children playing a game at the table. Charlie was right there with them. True, he was not really participating, but he was quietly watching everything. I felt much better. Then, Charlie looked up and saw me at the door. He got up from his chair and ran toward me, shrieking. The teacher was not able to muffle her annoyed expression fast enough. She came after Charlie and dragged him away from me. "I guess I'd better just go," I said, retreating backwards down the hall. This time the screaming continued until I was out the door.

I suppose Charlie's first day of school was no more traumatic than any other child's, and I doubt I cried more than any other mother. But, this time, underneath all the sadness and the avalanche of guilt, there was a flicker of hope. As much as it hurt, it was right.

With Charlie squared away at school, it was time to start concentrating on finding a job. I had a plan of action. As long as I was seeking new employment, why not better myself in the bargain? My resume was prepared, I had even sent copies to several employers I thought would, or should, be very excited to receive it. Now, I was ready to call on them personally and answer the questions that had been burning in their minds all these days. I'm sure that I subconsciously expected to find my resume sitting on the desk in front of the fortunate personnel manager who had been chosen to receive it.

By now, you must be aware that this was not to be the case. I rarely got to see anyone beyond the most junior member of the personnel staff. If they could locate my letter and resume, it was often buried in a crumpled folder containing other unsolicited offers to turn their company around. When mine was pulled out, it usually looked as if someone had eaten their lunch on it.

As the first jobless month drew to a close, we began cutting back. Charlie's school had found some part-time typing for me to do. It helped ease the worry about money a bit. Many nights after Charlie was tucked away in bed, I stayed up reworking my budget. The cutbacks became slashes and gouges. I read the want ads more carefully, including the ads for the lower paying jobs. These I had ignored at first, convinced that I could do better. But as the days passed, my expectations lowered. If I could just get a reasonable permanent job, then I could work my way up. What worried me most was health insurance. Living with a child and no health insurance is like living with a time bomb.

After late nights of planning and worrying, I looked tired every morning. It was becoming more difficult to look confident and capable at interviews. I noticed that my voice became more like a monotone as I repeated the same answers to the same questions day after day. It took longer each time to get ready for an interview. I would sit in the car outside the building I was to go into and pump myself up—"You came here for a good reason and you are not going back defeated. Smile. Back straight. And, for God's sake don't cross your legs and lean forward with your shoulders all hunched and wrinkled when you are in there. If you look desperate, they'll think there is a reason no one else has hired you. Now, for Charlie, get this job."

One more interview and then one more, "Thank you for your time. We'll be in touch."

Some mornings, if I wasn't working at school, I dropped Charlie off and went home to pore over the newspaper and make phone calls. It seemed so pointless. By now, I had caught onto the euphemisms of employment ads. I knew that "grow with the position" meant starting at the bottom. "Salary commensurate with experience" meant that if they printed how low the salary was, no one would call for an interview. If they were looking for a "self-starter," it meant the job was so boring that you had to motivate yourself to stay awake.

I began driving to Charlie's school before going on a job interview. I would take one run through the campus. It reminded me of why I was doing this and why I could not give up. It seemed to give me some strength. I continued the practice, hoping it would bring me luck.

But luck was not to be with me. Charlie's classmates were sharing the chicken pox, and Charlie, naturally, joined in. I was told he would have to stay home for two weeks. This was the final blow. Now, I had to stay home from even my part-time work. When I called my mother to lament my lot, she reminded me that if I were working, staying home with a sick child for two weeks would really be a problem. "Better he gets these things over with now." Better for whom? The unkindest cut of all was that Charlie was not the least bit sick. Apart from those ghastly spots all over his face and body, he felt fine. No fever, no fatigue. Two weeks of trying to keep him entertained was more than my sorely depleted patience could stand. I couldn't look for a job because no one with any kids wanted to keep Charlie for fear of contamination. So, we lived in quarantine while I watched my savings, my patience, and my hope dry up. The only thing that wasn't drying up was Charlie's chicken pox. It lasted the whole two weeks.

With no one to talk to (no one, that is, who could talk back), I turned to monologue.

"Well, what are you going to do? Go back?"
"What would be the difference? I would still be without a job."

"*Your family would help. Maybe you could get your old job back.*"

"*Fine. And what do I do with Charlie? Leave him here? The one thing about this move that has worked is Charlie's being in a good school.*"

"*It won't do him much good if he's so hungry he can't sit up at his desk.*"

"*He gets lunch at school. I'll just tell him to sneak an extra roll into his pocket to bring home to his mother.*"

"*With your luck, he would bring you pudding in his coat pocket.*"

"*Very funny. How about a useful suggestion for a change.*"

"*Hey, wait. You had better not make me angry. I'm the only help you have right now.*"

"*You're right. Let's pull ourselves together. We've got to make some plans, now. Serious, desperate plans.*"

"*Is this going to be another budget meeting, or will we just make more 'Things I Have to Do' lists?*"

"*We are going to respond to every want ad for every job that sounds reasonable and moral. Then, we'll work our way up later. If this town thinks it can run me off . . .*"

"*. . . or starve you out . . .*"

"*. . . it had better think again. They are dealing with a MOTHER. There is nothing so ferocious in nature as a mother protecting her young.*"

"*If this is going to be another pep rally, I think I'd rather make lists.*"

During the two-week siege of the chicken pox, I answered every ad for every job in town. I applied for jobs for which I was not even remotely qualified, although my letters sounded as though I had done that very job for years. I pulled out every stop. I even wrote to post office boxes for ads with no job description except the word *secretary*. I don't know how much of my desperation at this point was based on the fear of having to stay home every day with Charlie.

The only place I took Charlie during the chicken pox was to buy food and stamps. By this time, though, I really didn't care who he infected with chicken pox. If the town was not willing to give me a chance, then being ravaged with chicken pox was just punishment.

On the Thursday night of the second week, I sat on the floor by the telephone. I wanted to talk to an old friend, to someone I knew, but feared the long distance bill. I figured that I had one more alternative. It was a desperate action. If I were *gone*, Charlie could at least have the benefit of my estate, such as it was. Someone would take care of him. He was so gorgeous, he would be adopted right away if someone in the family didn't take him. Then, at least, he could grow up away from the shadow of a failure of a mother. I began to cry. Once started, the sobs overtook me. I shook and sobbed until I could hardly breathe. "Help me," I called. The crying blotted out any attempt at rational thought. It held me and would not let go. "Leave us alone," I screamed, my face turned up to, what? If I could just wrench myself free from the wave after wave of ill fortune that kept pounding me, I could save us. If it or they would just let me.

When exhaustion finally brought an end to my hysteria, I felt unexpectedly calm. The next Monday, after Charlie went to school, I would do it. Someone would take care of him. Maybe with me gone, all these things would stop happening to hurt him. Tomorrow, I would think of the best way to do it, but now, I had to sleep.

The next morning, I silently got Charlie up and made his breakfast. I could barely see out of the swollen slits that were my eyes. I was still calm, though. The specifics on just what I would do that day to solve our problem were not in my thoughts. My mind focused totally on the activity of the moment. Each of the habitual motions of making coffee, pouring cereal into a bowl, and closing the refrigerator door consumed all of my attention and consciousness. "Set the bowl on the table just here. Walk to the drawer. Open the drawer. Take out a spoon. Two spoons." Some defense mechanism had taken over my brain and was not allowing me to think about anything except the action I was performing at that exact instant.

Charlie sat down to his breakfast as if it were any other day. He smiled at me, excited about another new day. He must have slept on his right side all night because his hair on that side stuck out. It flopped freely when he moved his head or when he walked. Normally, Charlie's *wing* made me laugh. Not today. Somehow unaware of my mood, or indifferent to it, Charlie ate his cereal while maintaining a soft, rhythmic humming beneath his crunching. He repeatedly left the table to look out the window or to check on his toy cars. On one return trip to the table, he brought several little cars with him. No toys at the table is one of my strictest rules, but today, I watched Charlie roll the cars around, over, and into his cereal bowl without saying anything.

After Charlie ate, I watched him play, without really seeing him. I was thinking. No very good methods for doing *it* came to mind. I had to find a way to avoid the grisly reality of someone finding me, or whatever would remain of me. But, there was time. Something would come to me before Monday.

The phone rang. I rose automatically and counted the steps into the bedroom to answer. "If you can come in this morning, we would like to talk to you about the resume that you sent in response to our ad."

I jerked upright. Thoughts flooded my mind. "What to wear. Who could I get to watch Charlie? What could I do about this hair? These puffy eyes?" The peace and calm were gone. Blood was pumping and wheels were turning. I took down the address and said I would be there later that morning. "I have a few other appointments this morning." (What am I saying? I'll take the job. Don't worry, I'm very smart, and you'll love me.) I hung up the phone and began walking in little circles around the bedroom. Charlie found this most amusing, and thinking it was a game, began to follow me. He made a dash for between my legs and I tripped. I had to laugh. I pulled myself up and told Charlie to go play with his cars.

Okay—What first? A sitter. Who could I get to watch him? I began to go through the little slips of paper in the drawer under the phone. Who could I call? Several different possibilities occurred to me at once. I began to sort them out. Then, I stopped for an instant and realized that I did not know which job this was. I had answered so many ads lately that I had lost track. The phone book, look up the name and address in the phone book. Here it is—attorneys. I had never worked for attorneys before. I thought a tort was a cake. I thought general counsel was a member of the Joint Chiefs. No matter. It was the first positive response I had had. If they wanted typing, they would get it. I may have had a master's degree, but one thing I had learned: you can't eat it, or wear it, or live in it. If typing would keep Charlie in school, then stand back and watch for the smoking carriage.

As soon as I could sit down without my legs propelling me back up, I called for a sitter. One of the teachers at Charlie's school said she thought her mother wouldn't mind watching him for an hour or two. I called her mother and explained that I wouldn't be long, just long enough for the interview. I also assured her that Charlie really was over the chicken pox. Just to make sure, I put a little makeup on the more obvious spots still remaining.

"I know you won't like this, Charlie, but please bear with me. If I can get this job, we'll be okay. Wouldn't it be nice to have a mother who was not depressed and hysterical for a change?"

Charlie didn't answer, but I felt sure that he would have agreed with me if he could. Yes, I left him with a complete stranger who did not know sign language, but desperate times call for desperate measures. So what if he was miserable for an hour. Landing a job would keep me from being miserable all the time. The dear woman who watched Charlie told me repeatedly not to worry. I left thanking her a bit more profusely than was necessary.

The interview went well, I suppose. Everything was negotiable by this point. When the interview was over, I felt like I should have paid a cashier. But, I was assured of a decision that very day. No more waiting was certainly the best news of all. And, if the answer was no, well, then I guess I would keep looking. For some reason the alternative that had seemed the only option last night and this morning did not occur to me now. Surely, if I kept negotiating down all of my expectations, someone would hire me. I just hoped it would be before I got to the point where I was offering to do everything for free.

That afternoon, Charlie and I took a nap. I was exhausted from the rigors of the night before and the anxiety of the morning. The phone ringing woke me. I bolted up in bed. Charlie continued sleeping peacefully beside me. (I envy the oblivion his deafness affords him at times.) The phone call was from one of the attorneys. He offered me the job, which I accepted very coolly. "Come in Monday? Well, I suppose that will be all right." When I hung up the phone, I shook Charlie awake. I dragged him up with me and held his hands as we jumped on the bed. He was still groggy from the nap, but the jumping soon woke him up. "Mama has a job. A real job, with health insurance." I said the last word solemnly. Charlie did not understand about the job, but he loved the jumping on the bed. This was another forbidden activity I would later regret having allowed.

Being a secretary in a law office was not what I had hoped for. I thought it was a step down from what I had left. But it was a start, and the blessed health insurance would eliminate that fear of the unexpected. We weren't exactly on our way up the ladder, but we did have our hands on the bottom rung. Even if we were swinging just a bit, at least we had something to hold onto. I would swing and kick and pull and cling to that rung until I could reach the next one and pull Charlie up with me.

When the anxiety of looking for a job had passed and I had settled into my new routine, I found a new situation begging for a solution—the dormitory. How large it loomed before me, like some giant looking down at me with mocking eyes, mouth gaping wide to devour my son. I knew from the beginning that the school was a residential institution. Most schools for the deaf are. They must be, for children come from all over the state to attend. Their parents cannot all leave jobs or farms or businesses to move to the town where the school is located. In times past, handicapped children were sent away to be housed and raised by the state or private concerns. The image of stern matrons with iron faces watching over cowering unfortunates, I have found, dies hard.

I had no intention of having Charlie stay in the dormitory when I moved him to his new school. My image was of the two of us beaming through the days, hand in hand. He would wave cheerfully as he boarded the bus to school, and I would wave back equally elated to be off to another day of satisfying work. We would meet at night and sign enthusiastically about our day's adventures over a light but nutritious evening meal. Then, an evening of constructive play together before a fun-filled bath and kiss good night. Is it ever thus?

What really happened was that I had to leave for work too early to allow Charlie to ride the school bus. So, I took him to school. The other children were usually still at breakfast, so Charlie sat in the cafeteria and watched them or waited in the dorm lounge for their return. In the afternoon, of course, he could stay at school and play until I came to pick him up. That was after the children with mothers at home had long gone on the bus. By the time I got off work, the resident children were again in the cafeteria, this time having dinner. Or, if some outing had been planned, they were all gone. On those days, I retrieved Charlie from the infirmary where he sat, not unattended but basically alone, waiting for his work-weary mother. I would find him sitting on a bench, his school bag clutched at the ready, watching the door. It is an image I see yet, and which then made me question myself daily.

The dormitory staff was sympathetic to my situation and made all sorts of concessions to my schedule. They suggested that Charlie eat dinner with the other kids. This he enjoyed. It meant I had dinner alone, or I skipped dinner (which didn't hurt me), or Charlie ate twice (which apparently didn't hurt him). Sometimes Charlie would be invited to go out with the dorm kids on a picnic or for a hamburger. Then, I came for him in the evening. It seemed as if Charlie was becoming more and more involved in the residential program, yet he was coming home with me to sleep. He seemed to be enjoying dorm life. I noticed subtle changes in his behavior. He had more of a sense of sharing, of being responsible, of being part of a group. The staff and superintendent encouraged me to let Charlie stay in the dorm through the week. I refused to consider it, even though he was practically living there already.

The evenings at home with Charlie in no way resembled my image of a blissful life. Tired from a day of service, I usually felt little inclination toward exemplary motherhood. The constructive activities were begun with the best of intentions but given up before much progress was made. Charlie was usually restless from so much waiting, and he became bored with me. So, after some embarrassing excuse for dinner, I was left with a son nagging for attention but with few resources for keeping him entertained.

The legion of friends in our apartment building that Charlie was to assemble later had not been formed as yet. Now, his friends were all at school and being home with me was boring. However, our life together was not. Something was always happening to confound one or both of us.

Driving, particularly for extended periods of time, can be a grueling experience for any parent. No child's attention span can outlast a trip of more than a few minutes. However, when conversation is removed as a passer of time and occupier of mind, the options for entertainment are seriously diminished. When Charlie and I finally moved from my parent's home, we made weekend visits. The car ride was of several hours' duration. The excitement of seeing Grandma and Grandpa again kept Charlie awake all the way there. He flitted from front seat to back, alternating between playing with his toys and looking out the window. At first, the drive was excruciating for me. The problems started just after sunset, when Charlie became anxious, fidgety, demanding, and generally obnoxious. He poked me on the shoulder constantly to get my attention. Being poked every few minutes for three or four hours would try anyone's patience, I suspect. But, that was nothing compared to having to jerk my head around so that Charlie could sign to me from the back seat.

On one of these trips, for some long-forgotten reason, I turned on the dome light in the car. Almost at once, Charlie calmed down. Sitting beside me, he could easily sign to me. I was overwhelmed by my lack of awareness, once again. Driving at night with the inside light on is not the most pleasant way to travel a major headache is soon developed. However, for Charlie, it meant the continuation of communication. He was a little less isolated, and he could share his enjoyment of the trip. It did not solve the problem of the jerked head. That had to wait until Charlie learned to sign to me in the rearview mirror.

Parents of hearing children fail to see the great luxury they are afforded in being able to call to their children from a distance. In my more idealistic days (which means premotherhood), I cringed at hearing, "Billy, come home now," shouted from a window or porch. However, chasing my child across a yard or down a store aisle to get his attention strikes me as equally undignified. As soon as Charlie learned to look at my face to communicate, he also learned that closing his eyes kept away any unwanted messages, such as "bedtime" or "stop that." More than once I have spent humiliating minutes chasing Charlie around in circles, trying to get in front of him to tell him something. Seeing me try to maneuver my way into his line of vision must be like watching a cat chase its tail. It feels much the same, I suspect.

Losing sight of a deaf child in a public place is frightening. I have spent some frantic minutes, even halves of hours, trekking up and down store aisles looking for a missing Charlie. The initial few minutes are given to anger—"Why did I let him get away from me?" The next few minutes lead to embarrassment because I have passed the same clerks and shoppers five or six times by now. Finally, I move into a panic—"Charlie would not be able to ask anyone for help. What if he left the store and is wandering helplessly in the parking lot?" Mercifully, this hasn't happened yet. Once, though, I exceeded frantic and was nearly in tears when I found Charlie pedaling a tricycle through the television section of a K-Mart. The store personnel were not amused. As I recall, I abandoned my shopping cart and fled the premises.

One Saturday shortly after Charlie and I moved into our own apartment, I indulged myself in a morning shower. Charlie was busy playing in his room, in his underwear, not feeling the necessity to dress until threatened to do so or until he could somehow arrange to have me do it for him. When I emerged from the shower, berobed and betoweled, Charlie was not in the apartment. I had not sufficiently terrorized him about going out the front door without me. I raced to the window prepared to see a crowd in the parking lot gathered around a flattened child. They would all suddenly turn, in unison, and point their fingers at me, the guilty mother selfish enough to take a shower on her son's time.

What I saw was a boy in his underwear sitting blissfully on the hood of my car. Relieved that he had survived the crossing of the parking lot, I resolved to make him regret it. Dilemma. Should I take the time to throw on some clothes and risk his further wandering? I opted to rescue him for his execution thus attired. It was at that precise time that the majority of my neighbors were either going to or coming from their cars. I strode out, grabbed my progeny and returned as quickly as dignity would allow. Happily, the wind was calm, preventing a robe incident. The more fortunate mother of a hearing child could have discreetly bellowed from the window, "Charlie, get in this house so I can kill you. And, be careful crossing the parking lot."

A further note on the subject of cars and crossings. I have always seen cars as a source of great danger to Charlie. No child watches very diligently for oncoming cars when playing or crossing streets. But, hearing children at least have the benefit of a warning system. They can hear the oncoming car, or its horn, or the driver making threats against their lives. Not so for Charlie. Engrossed in play, it might be easy for him to wander off into the parking lot on his tricycle, just as it is for any child. With his back turned, a car could be on him without warning.

I decided the way to meet this problem was to instruct Charlie in the proper behavior around cars. He would not fully understand the danger, perhaps, but if the behavior were drilled into him, it might save him from disaster. So, each time we came to a street corner or the end of the parking lot, I signed, "Stop." We had to both stop at once. I looked first one direction and then another. "Look" is signed with the fingers of both hands in a *v* position. The tips of the *v* fingers go to the eyes and then out toward whatever one is looking at. So, I turned my fingers to the right and then to the left. "Look for cars," I repeated to Charlie. He pointed his fingers and moved his body in perfect imitation of me.

After many repetitions, I decided to give him the responsibilty. He had to look and tell when it was time to cross. We stopped. "You look for cars," I told him. My hands went to my sides. His did, too. "Charlie, look for cars," I said, and reminded him how to do it. Again, when my hands went down so did his. I grabbed his arm, shot a quick glance to see if the path was clear and dragged him across the street. Next attempt: "Charlie, look for cars." I folded my arms across my chest and donned an expression of irresponsibility. He started to cross the street. "Stop. Charlie, look for cars." Again, I crossed my arms. Now he understood. (The old broad is making me do all the work as usual, he probably thought.) Okay. Up went the fingers, his eyes glued on me to check for approval. His fingers moved right, then left. "Cross," he signed and started across the street. Of course, there was a car coming, and I jerked him back. "No, you goof. Look with your eyes, not your fingers." I pointed (jabbing) at my eyes. Charlie pointed to his eyes. "Charlie, look for cars." His eyes riveted on my face, he stuck his fingers out in front of him and shot a quick right-left. "No, look with your eyes." I helped him move his head, assuming his eyes would follow. When I looked down, they were shut tight. Obviously, I had led us into this quagmire of misunderstanding. I took charge again and got us across the street. We started over to the next corner, and both of us looked for cars.

I spent much uncomfortable time in the quagmire of misunderstanding. Misunderstandings are sources of frustration and humiliation, for me anyway. I am usually the one who mis-understands and the one who ends up feeling the worst. Not infrequently, it is the result of a poorly executed sign.

A prime example of misunderstanding happened one morn-ing as we were finally ready to go out the door. As usual, Charlie had dawdled through his breakfast and getting dressed to the point where we were beyond delayed, past unpunctual, and well into late. I was loaded down with encumbrances. Charlie made a grab for my keys. The door was locked and needed only to have the deadbolt latch turned to open. I positioned my burdens so that I could sign, "Unlock the door." Charlie's hands were poised on the latch, but on seeing my signs, they dropped. "Unlock the door," I repeated, emphasizing each sign for clarity. Charlie took a step back. That look of "What is Mom going to do to me now?" crept over his face. My voice rose and I signed in quick, jabbing gestures, "Unlock the door." Charlie began to cry and he dropped the keys. I snatched them up, unlocked the door, dropped what I was carrying, and shoved him out the door. He followed obediently at my heels, and, in a final blus-tering flourish, we got in the car.

As I turned the key in the ignition, I realized that I had signed *don't* for *un*. A reasonable association for an adult. But, for Charlie, the sign meant *don't*. He had seen it often. The sign for lock and key are very close. *Key* he knew; *lock* he probably didn't. He saw me say, "Don't key the door," instead of "Unlock the door." He wasn't keying the door, and still I persisted. He had moved back to indicate that he most definitely was not keying the door. I became angrier. He dropped the keys so there could be absolutely no possibility of his keying the door. Then, I grabbed the keys, further confirming that I was talking about keys, and I shoved Charlie out the door. As this series of associa-tions was playing itself out in my brain, Charlie was cowering in the car seat beside me. I turned off the engine and looked at him. I could not possibly explain my mistake. I said, "I'm sorry," and we hugged. He was unsure at first, but we ended up in a tight embrace and I left yet another of my tears on his cheek.

Misunderstandings between children and the rest of the world occur all the time. Even with hearing children. One of the myopias of parents of deaf children (or at least of this one) is that we tend to view all problems in terms of the handicap. Charlie likes to go skating. He enjoys the activity at the rink, and so we go sometimes. Mama's skating ability is meager at best, but we go. Once, I was fortunate enough to con a friend into going along who could keep us both on our feet. The unfortunate part is that she had her own skates. Why unfortunate? Because Charlie and I were renters, and as with all things rented, the skates had to be returned. As the end of a rollicking skating spree, Charlie became adamant about taking his skates home. As far as he knew, we had paid for them. (Try explaining that seventy-five cents does not a pair of skates buy.) Our friend got to take her skates home. And so a fight ensued. When the manager of the rink, who happened to be in the vicinity, saw me trying to pry the skates from the hands of my screaming child, I began to explain. "Charlie is deaf, and he is a little confused about the skates."

"He wants to take them home, huh?"

"That's right. The idea of renting is a bit beyond his language at this point."

"That's okay. All the little ones want to take their skates home. Why not? They saw Mama pay for them, so they think the skates belong to them now."

I smiled back, sheepishly, and with a final jerk, freed the skates from Charlie's grasp. I was grateful that he didn't realize just how stupid I was feeling. I wondered if I would ever get used to being wrong about Charlie. Not only that, but I had this feeling of having given away Charlie's *bad news* needlessly. Not that it was something I tried to hide, or could have. It's just that admitting it unnecessarily made me angry at myself.

Sometimes I have been left to wonder how certain things happened. If Charlie was unable to tell me, I, of course, suspected the worst. A chain of pizza establishments has made its fortune by being considerate enough to furnish entertainment while customers wait to be served. Instead of drumming fingers on a table, we are given a whole host of arcade games to explore. Charlie loved this place; he could work his way through his own weight in quarters before a small pizza baked.

Once, on an excursion to this parental purgatory, Charlie left me at the table to finish eating while he went back to the games. Grateful for the relative quiet, but rationalizing that this was a good independent activity for him, I let him go. Tied to his arm was a yellow balloon, purchased with the first of the afternoon's quarters. I had had to bat it away from my face each time I tried to take a bite of pizza. No matter, we were having fun.

When Charlie returned a few minutes later for another quarter (a very few minutes later) he was carrying a blue balloon. "Where is the yellow balloon?"

"Gone," he replied.

"Gone where?"

"Gone."

The balloon machine was the one machine I doubted that Charlie could work alone, but maybe he had had help. No, the balloon machine took two quarters, and Charlie had left me with only one. I tried again. "Where is the yellow balloon?"

"Gone."

Quickly listing the possibilities in my mind, I arrived at four explanations. One: Someone had felt sorry for Charlie trying to get a balloon with only one quarter and had given him another. (What kind of mother would send her child to the balloon machine with only one quarter?) Two: Charlie's balloon had broken and someone bought him another. (Where is the poor, unhappy child's mother?) Three: He had seen a child with a blue balloon and traded. (What a little charmer, but where is his mother?) Four (I saved the worst until last, although it was the possibility that occurred to me first): Charlie had seen a child with a blue balloon and offered to trade. The child had refused, so Charlie had punched him and taken the blue balloon. There was a child lying in the arcade with a yellow balloon hovering above him to mark the spot. (Where is the mother of this little tyrant?) Fearing formal charges by the other child's mother and the restaurant, I gathered my things and we headed for the door, the blue balloon giving us away. I never did discover the answer to the great balloon switch, and no one has called to investigate.

I have delivered my share of zingers in embarrassing situations. Once, pulling up to the carryout lane at the supermarket to pick up groceries, the young man loading my car said, "Hi, there," to Charlie. He received no response, of course. "Hi," he tried again, still unsuccessful. The boy looked at me and shrugged, "A little spaced out today, eh?"

"No, he's deaf," I answered smugly.

"Oh." If I had remembered Charlie's hearing aid, the boy's chagrin would have been avoided. The sack boy would probably never speak to another customer, lose his job, be forced to quit school, and wind up on the street thanks to my colossal lack of tact.

While on the subject, I may as well confess to my own contribution to salesperson anxiety. It began innocently enough. Since discovering the trick, I have pulled it whenever I've been in a particularly devilish mood.

Stores like to make one final attempt at a sale by placing items tempting to a child at the checkout stands. What mother has not fought with her child over some trinket dangling in plain view? When I find myself in this predicament, I try to maintain my privacy by signing to Charlie without talking. Why should everyone around me know that I am refusing to buy my child something he clearly wants? We sign without talking and when my turn comes to have my grocery cart totaled, the clerk hesitates. She does not greet me with the company amenity, "How are you today?" or "Did you find everything?" She begins silently to add up my damages. Aha! She thinks I am deaf and is probably wondering how she will tell me what amount to pay. I let her worry, signing again to Charlie to increase her anxiety. Then, just as the last item comes out of the cart, I say something like, "It sure is busy today," or "Can you believe this weather?" The look on the clerk's face is priceless. The only free thing in the store. Relief, embarrassment, all rolled into one. A double treat. I rationalize my inexcusable behavior by telling myself that I have made the clerk more aware of and sensitive to the needs of a deaf customer, and I have given her an opportunity to prepare her response.

A fascinating variation on this same theme of being mistaken for deaf occurs when people think I don't hear them talking about us. Restaurants are the best places for this. People are held captive in one spot for a considerable period with a whole menagerie on display before them. A feast for the eye and the ear. I make sure that Charlie and I are seated wordlessly. By the time people notice us, we are into a sign conversation. Again, for purposes of privacy, I do not use my voice, but merely form the words with my mouth. With my peripheral vision, I see people watching us. Pretty soon, I catch snatches of conversation.

"We really ought to persuade Uncle Ned to get a hearing aid. He's becoming almost deaf."

"Is that little boy wearing a hearing aid? Can you imagine that? They make them for little kids."

"Look, Mom, that kid has a little radio. Can I have one, too?"

Of course, the most entertaining people are those who expound their considerable knowledge of deafness.

"I read where deaf people are able to get some kind of captions on their TV shows."

"Yes. I read something about those in a magazine."

"I've never seen any captions on my TV."

"I think you have to be looking right at the TV to see them; you know, real close."

"No, you have to have a special kind of TV. Or else, I think you need a special antenna to get them."

"Oh."

"Yeah. Then, up in the corner there is a person talking sign language so the deaf person knows what's going on."

How tempting it is to turn around and say, "No, actually it's not a special antenna, and the captions are printed words across the bottom of the screen." Usually in these situations, I keep up the pretense as long as possible. It does delay service sometimes. I have visions of waitresses flipping a coin; the loser gets to wait on us.

Sometimes, of course, we do run into deaf people. They are never fooled. They can tell by my pidgin signs that I can hear. They always speak to us; that is, they sign to us. I always love to see Charlie's reaction. His face lights up whenever someone signs to him. He becomes shy and then he smiles without saying anything, but he is clearly pleased for someone to talk to him in his own language. After they have walked on, Charlie will run after them and tell them something of great import like, "See my grapes." That experience always reconvinces me that Charlie must have contact with his people, and he must learn how to get along with mine.

The slowness of a deaf child's language development is sometimes surprising to the uninformed. I have frequently seen the incredulous look of someone who asked Charlie's age. Clearly they were impressed with his ability to sign. Yet, if they could have understood our communication they might have been just as surprised at its primitiveness. My conversations with five-year-old Charlie were on the language level of a much younger child. He was stuck, temporarily, in a me-Tarzan-you-Jane stage.

Why so slow? Language is learned by rote. Ask anyone who has learned a foreign language. Words, singly and then grouped together into ever more complex patterns, must be memorized. There is no way to conceptualize language so that new vocabulary is reasoned. For example, young children make grammatical mistakes when they try to generalize rules to new words. *I walk, I walked* leads to *I go, I goed*. The correct *I went* must be memorized. More proof: We have all heard a phrase which we know to be incorrect without knowing why. *I seen her before* sounds wrong to us. We may have, at some point, learned the grammatical rule that the past perfect tense includes the proper form of the verb *to have*. Correct usage is *I have seen (had, will have, would have,* etc.*) her before.*" We may not know the grammatical reason for this error, but knowing that it is an error goes back much farther, to the time we heard and memorized language patterns.

In order for a child to memorize a word or phrase, it must be repeated many times. For hearing children this is easy. They are bombarded with language all the time. It is there for the taking, whether they are paying attention or not. For deaf children, the repetitions of a word register only when they are paying attention; when it is directed right at them, in good light; and when they understand the word in the first place. Clearly, the more difficult operation. And, this only comes after a child has learned to look at the speaker's face and knows what words actually are.

Trying to teach language to a deaf child when you both are also engaged in everyday activities creates new challenges. At first, nouns can only be taught in relation to concrete objects. Concepts such as verbs and adjectives come much later. Suppose you want to teach the word *hot;* a rather useful word. Hearing children can be appropriately terrorized with threats—"Your hand will turn black and crispy if you touch the stove." Definitely grisly, but way beyond a deaf toddler's grasp. So, one must threaten the child not to come near the stove, or else . . . something. It may seem arbitrary to a child. How can an item so closely resembling a benign washing machine be capable of such pain? This can be either the pain caused by the stove itself or by some punishment imposed by Mother. Now, of course, hearing children, too, can be skeptical of such things. They may need to learn the hard way. But, at least theoretically, they have other options.

Beyond the teaching of words, there is the difficulty of communication itself. Deaf children must be physically approached for communication to take place. No matter where they wander, you have to hunt them down and get their attention by putting yourself in their line of vision. Sometimes, in an effort to avoid going all the way outside, I have stood at the door vigorously flapping my arms in the hope of catching a bit of Charlie's peripheral vision. Not a very dignified sight.

If you rely on your hands for communication, it is essential that they remain free. However, everyday chores do not always allow such freedom. I have often loaded myself with purse,

114

lunch, umbrella, and newspaper, preparing to leave home for work, and then noticed Charlie's shoes lying forsaken on the floor. Even a simple, "Put on your shoes," requires me to unload, sign, reload. At least, to my credit, I have learned to wait for a response from Charlie before I pick everything up again.

Another mental picture at which I shudder is that of me holding two grocery bags, standing in front of a closed door. While I have little doubt that Charlie can read "Open the door" on my lips, logic should tell him this has to be done. Still, he looks at me with his most charming "I don't understand" expression, until I set down both bags and sign. Of course, by the time I pick up the bags again he has opened the door and gone through. Now, I'm standing heavy laden in front of a closed door, and Charlie is on the other side with his back to me.

Even Charlie had some difficulty manipulating play and signing at first. When he was very small I had to stand in front of him on the swings to push him. Then, I could sign, "Higher?" or "Look at Charlie," or some other inane parental chatter. Charlie, of course, could not answer without letting go of the swing. He had to learn to make a good one-handed *stop* sign, which took me several tries to figure out.

Privacy is generally a luxury for anyone who lives with children. More so for the single mother. For me, it became all but the impossible dream. Every mother knows that her entering the bathroom signals open season on all previously unthinkable mischief. From the tranquility of the two-minute shower she hears, "Mom, can we bring the hose in through the window and make a water bed? We've already got all the spongy stuff out of the mattress." She, at least, can run out in time to keep irreparable destruction from being wrought. However, there is no communicating with a deaf child through a closed bathroom door. The child either will knock until you manage to open, or, if you are not prompt enough, will assume silence means consent. "Look Mom, I decided to pour my own milk." The drip of a gallon of milk from table to floor is imperceptible from behind a closed bathroom door, I assure you.

Wherever we have lived, Charlie has become acquainted with our neighbors before I have. He is not made shy by his handicap; on the contrary, he is quite gregarious. Most people think he is adorable (which he is), and of course, he's helpful and courteous to anyone who is not his own mother.

Often, my first encounter with people in my apartment building came when they were conversing successfully with Charlie. It was just such a chance meeting that led to Charlie's being "healed." I had gone out to look for Charlie and had found him conversing with a young, eager-looking couple. We exchanged hellos as I tried to encourage-cajole-bribe-threaten Charlie up to our apartment for lunch. A few minutes after I had succeeded, the doorbell rang.

"Hello, again."

"Hello."

"We couldn't help noticing . . . is that a hearing aid your son is wearing?"

"Yes, it is," I answered, cringing at the obvious question.

"Is he very deaf?"

(How deaf would you like?) "Yes, he has a profound loss," I answered, becoming bored with this line of inquiry from strangers at my own door.

"Have you asked God to heal him?"

"Many times. So far, no luck."

"Would you mind if we just came in for a minute. I'd like to tell you about another deaf boy that we saw the Lord heal."

"Actually, I don't really go in for that sort of thing," I said, feeling subtlety would be wasted on these unkempt, but otherwise polite zealots.

"Won't you let us try?"

"If it won't take long." (Why not?) Charlie had been sitting at the kitchen table during this exchange. It was summer and he had chosen jogging shorts, chest au naturel, knee socks, and cowboy boots for his ensemble that day. Thus bedecked, he was engaged in eating crackers and peanut butter. More correctly, he

116

was building a stack of crackers and peanut butter. Each little sandwich he made, using one-quarter cup of peanut butter to two saltines, was added to a growing stack. Most of these would be stored for several days in plastic wrap and eventually thrown away, but it was a good dexterity exercise for him, and it could guarantee quiet for as long as fifteen minutes. Half a jar of peanut butter was a small price to pay for quiet, by my account.

The sight of people at the door brought Charlie down from his chair. He took the young man's arm in greeting and pulled him inside. Then, as if remembering what he had abandoned, he returned to the table.

"What a beautiful boy. I'm sure we can help him," the young man said, running through his longish hair a hand that looked like it should have been fixing a car or laying asphalt instead of healing the infirm.

"Listen," I said, "I happen to have heard about this boy who was 'cured,' from some people I know. I know that his loss was much less than Charlie's."

"Nothing is too great for God's hand." I managed to catch my eyes in midroll.

"Are you familiar with the Scriptures?" the young man asked. So far, the woman with him had said nothing. She was dressed in a style complementary to the man, or perhaps those were the man's clothes. While the young man talked to me, the woman spent her time looking around my apartment. For future reference? I wondered.

"Yes, I am familiar with the Bible." By this time, Charlie had resumed his seat at the table and was intently trying to reach the bottom of the peanut butter jar with his knife. He offered a little sandwich to the visitors. The woman looked at her companion, wondering, I suppose, if the Lord would let her take it. He took one, saying how sweet it was for Charlie to share, but I could tell from his expression that he was hardly prepared to eat such a mess, even for the Lord. This lifted my estimation of him, somewhat. He did not acknowledge his companion's rather imploring expression.

"Listen," I said again, in an effort to speed things up. "I appreciate your concern and your beliefs, but I can't help you. This is between you, Charlie, and God." (So get to it.)

Feeling their opportunity slipping, the couple began to pray, accompanied by the sound of Charlie's crunching. Then, they both placed their hands on Charlie's head and beseeched God to give Charlie back the hearing that the devil had stolen from him. As the praying became more intense, the young woman began to sway. Perhaps this was the part for which she had been brought along. Charlie's head was by now pushed nearly to the table top. He looked up at me as best he could without moving his head and gave me a very puzzled expression. I shrugged. It was an effort for him to continue eating his snack, but he did so, gallant lad. The couple began talking in unintelligible sounds, while Charlie still chomped away. Then, together, they lifted their hands and brought themselves back to their own version of reality.

"He is healed," the young man announced. I looked at Charlie with some care. He had brought himself back to an upright position and was testing the movement remaining in his neck. There was no noticeable difference in Charlie, except for a slight thickening of the peanut butter in the corners of his mouth. My skepticism must have showed.

"He is healed, but you may not notice the change for a while. It may even take a couple of days, but I feel that God has worked a miracle for Charlie." At this point, the woman involuntarily let go a "Praise the Lord," and the man looked around at her. She drew back.

I got up from the kichen chair and began walking toward the door, hoping they would follow me. I thanked them, of course. When we made it to the door, I held it open for their exit. The young believers were telling me about their church. Mercifully, at that moment, the phone rang. My eyes flew to Charlie for a response (even I hope), but there was none. I looked at the couple, who obviously had missed the significance of this "sign." It did, however, give me an excuse to close (and lock) the door. I signed, "Telephone," to Charlie so he would know where I was going, and headed for the bedroom to answer it.

For the next couple of days, Charlie took great delight in sneaking up on me from behind and putting his hands, however sticky, on the top of my head and squeezing his eyes shut tight.

The eager couple did not return, either to check on their patient or to invite me to their church. Charlie, of course, continued to wear his hearing aid around the building, and perhaps that is what kept them away. Within a few weeks, they had moved, no doubt shaking the dust from their feet as they went.

7

One of the things I had not bargained for when I became the mother of a deaf child was other people's reactions to me and Charlie. Some feel amazingly free to offer their advice (which I've expounded on already). Others ask inane questions, and still others just stare. Being stared at is something to which I have become rather accustomed. Charlie catches the attention of the public because he is usually being chased by me. Once I catch up with him, it is the tap on the shoulder that gives us away. As I sign to him, either in the slashing gestures and intense facial expressions of a scolding or with the exaggeration of silliness, people watch. Even if we are talking more calmly, we draw the attention of those around us. It is interesting to watch people sign. I do it myself, though I can rarely keep up with the rapid-fire communication of adults.

Sometimes people comment, "What a darling little boy," or some other compliment. "Does he understand you when you talk with your hands?"

"Of course. He signs very well." Charlie's hands immediately fall limp at his sides. He was shy for a long time about signing in public, particularly when I had just told someone how well he could do it.

"How do you teach that to a child?" This one surprises me. Are they skeptical about how Spanish-speaking children learn Spanish so young? One learns one's own language from one's parents. It's the same process no matter what the language.

Another comment I frequently get from interested strangers is, "I always wanted to learn sign language. It must have taken you a long time to learn."

"We're learning together," is my standard reply.

"I don't know if I could get my hands to move like that, though."

"You would if you had to." They usually walk off about then.

"Can he hear at all with his hearing aid?" people often ask. A logical question.

My answer used to be, "Yes, the aid helps him hear some environmental sounds, but it does not let him hear speech." This explanation proved too lengthy for most curious passers-by. Besides, most people couldn't define *environmental sounds* readily. I took to answering this question by saying, "Some."

How much information Charlie gets from sound or through vibration I am still uncertain, but he is using his residual hearing more all the time. Slamming doors, loud crashes, even a loud baby crying will often catch his attention. The first time he heard (or felt) a very loud thunder clap, his face lit up. He was not fearful. He didn't even seem to wonder what it was. He was too delighted with the new experience to even ask.

I would not want to be thought of as optimistic on this subject, however. Charlie does have a certain credibility problem when it comes to his pronouncement, "I hear it." On more than one occasion, I have had to ask Charlie to be quiet. His pounding or screaming was not only annoying, but it threatened my status as a tenant in our apartment. When I tell him, "Loud. Hurts my ears," with a grimace, his face lights up and he tells me he can hear it. He already knows that I am so happy for him to hear something that chances are I will let him continue to pound, at least a few more strokes. The look on his face is strikingly similar to that he dons when conning me into letting him take just one toy to bed with him or leaving his dinner for his pudding.

I question his credibility not only because he is the devil personified, but also because he has made some very blatant errors with "I hear it." He has told me he could hear the car horn when the motor was off, when, in fact, the horn doesn't function. This was so he could sit on my lap and turn the lights on and off. He has also told me that he could hear the toaster, when what he wanted was to push the bread down for the third time. He even told me once he could hear a wooden ornamental knob on a piece of furniture when he turned it on. That was so he could climb up on the table to reach it.

That he does hear (or feel) some sound, though, I am convinced. The franchise pizza parlor with the arcade and mechanical animals, which became an important part of our weekend entertainment, is one such example. Charlie loves to listen to the animal band. I know that the volume has to be detrimental to normal hearing, but for Charlie, it is just right. When the music starts, Charlie descends from his seat and places my hands, palms down, on the table. Then, he climbs back up and positions himself the same way. We look as if we are having a seance, but I have seen him sit quietly in this position longer than in any other. For myself, I am good for only a few minutes before the pounding in my head becomes unbearable. Knowing that this is one of the few times when I am asked to endure discomfort for Charlie's listening enjoyment, I hold out as long as I can. When the cochlear demolition is unendurable, I can usually bribe him out of the room with a quarter and the promise of a game.

"Can he read lips, yet?" is the inevitable question. I confess that it has bothered me somewhat. It makes me ready to mount my mother-of-a-handicapped-child soapbox and regale them on lipreading. Actually, it's speechreading. I suppose the reason that particular question puts me off so is that the questioner assumes that Charlie will learn to depend on speechreading or that he should. Speechreading is not some kind of latent talent that we all inherit but which only develops in the deaf. It is a skill, one that is difficult to master. Even the best speechreaders lose between 50 and 60 percent of what they see. Add to that the individual speech idiosyncracies we all have. Some people barely move their lips when they speak. Some talk more out of one side of the mouth than the other. (I will resist the temptation to editorialize here.) Then, there are the smilers—nice, but hard to read. Clenched teeth, mustaches, and twitches all add to the difficulty of seeing what someone is saying.

Most people don't realize how many sounds and words look alike on the lips. Stand in front of a mirror and watch yourself say, without using your voice, *How now brown cow*. All the words look alike. Not only are there sounds that are indistinguishable by sight alone, some are invisible. The consonants produced in the back of the mouth or in the throat (e.g., *g, k, q*) and the nasal sounds (e.g., *n, ng*) are all invisible on the lips.

Deaf children learn speech by putting their hands on the face or throat of the speaker. They feel and then imitate those sounds. In polite society, however, it is not acceptable for a deaf person to feel a hearing person's face in order to catch the invisible sounds. The speechreader either guesses or loses these sounds.

The keys to successful speechreading are visibility and knowing the context of what is being said. How could you speechread a public speaker if you had to sit in the back of an audience? Try reading the speech of a television or movie character as he or she walks around, in and out of camera range. What about unseen narrators? Now ask me if Charlie can speechread yet.

The truth is, difficult as communication is with the hearing world, Charlie has always attempted it, and with great aplomb. He believes that everyone understands his signs. This has convinced me that Charlie does not realize that he is deaf and, therefore, different from most of the rest of the world.

Happy as I have been to see Charlie's adaptation to the hearing world and his obvious lack of inhibition, I confess that it has made me aware of the awakening that Charlie must face one day when he learns that he is not only different, but also very much in the minority in a hearing world. With that revelation will come questions, and big ones. *Why?* springs immediately to mind. That and having to pull baby teeth have made the future frightening indeed.

A more recent episode has convinced me that I need not fear Charlie's withdrawal from the hearing world. After an exhausting, whirlwind trip through the supermarket looking for, chasing, and scolding Charlie by turns, I waited for my turn to pay for my purchases. Daydreaming of how best to stretch hamburger into a week of fine dining, I lost track of Charlie for an instant. When I came to, he was gone. I began turning my head this way and that, like some mother bird looking for her young. Fearful of losing my place in line and, thus, my frozen food, I left my cart and stepped back for a wider view of the immediate area. Out of the corner of my eye I saw him at the express checkout. He was checking out with his bag of grapes and E.T. candy. The young woman at the cash register had rung up his purchase and was trying to tell him how much he must pay. Doubly futile. Even if Charlie had been able to hear her, he had no money.

Furious, I ran to Charlie's rescue. The reason we had come to this supermarket in midweek was that I had to write a check for cash. Now, I had to give up the little cash I had for grapes and E.T. candy. Express lanes should be equipped to take the checks of mothers whose children get away from them. Perhaps this was the store's subtle way of telling mothers to keep better track of their children. Whatever the reason, having taken care of Charlie's purchases I dragged him back to my abandoned cart, there to meet the scowls of the people stuck waiting behind it. Charlie inhibited by the hearing world? I think not. At least not when it offers him an opportunity to make a fool of his mother.

In addition to being Charlie's mother, chauffeur, playmate, cook, laundress, and friend, I have also been his interpreter. Charlie frequently has looked at me with a puzzled expression, as if to ask What's happening? What did she say? Other times, he has rebelled at my wanting to interject myself into his life. On one occasion, I wanted to accompany him to ask a friend to play. I tried to explain that I wanted to go along only to talk to Teddy's mother. She would have had difficulty communicating to Charlie that little Teddy couldn't play just now because they were expecting his grandmother or preparing to go out. Charlie resented my going and misunderstood my reasons. Was I going to interfere with his play in some way? Another of my daily dilemmas. It was important for Charlie to deal with social situations on his own. Yet, he clearly had not the resources to do so in many cases. He cried, of course. He refused to go to Teddy's unless I stayed home. I couldn't let him go and misunderstand Teddy's mother.

I stood in front of the door, blocking Charlie's exit until he relented and let me follow several paces behind him to Teddy's place.

When we arrived at Teddy's apartment, Charlie knocked. From inside I heard Teddy's mother. "That's Charlie. You can't play now, Teddy." She did not answer the door. While I understood completely her wish to avoid a difficult situation for Charlie as well as for herself, my maternal protectiveness flared. She was refusing to answer the door to *my* son. Not because Teddy couldn't play, but because Charlie couldn't hear. She found her own way to communicate. Charlie, of course, was not hurt. He believed Teddy was not home. Was Charlie deceived if he did not know of the deception? I felt the deception for him, even though I was part of it.

I do not expect everyone in the world to learn sign language for Charlie's benefit, though it would be nice. In the meantime, friends or relatives who see Charlie infrequently depend on me to interpret for them. Charlie depends on me, too. I really don't mind. It gives me a unique role in Charlie's life that no one else can fill. I'll make sure he remembers it when he grows up.

Once, when entertaining nonsigning guests, Charlie thought it would be more fun if we went to their house to visit. He said "Go to their house."

"What did he say?" one of our friends asked.

"Oh, he wants to go to your house to play."

"How sweet. You tell him to bring you and just come over any time he wants."

I told Charlie that we would go to their house later. Now, we would stay at Charlie's house. A loose translation, but sufficient.

After a couple of hours of being hugged, held, and generally harassed, Charlie tired of our guests' attention. He said to me, "They go home, now." His expression was so clear that I was afraid they would understand and be offended.

"What did he say?" came the inevitable question.

"Oh, he still wants to go to your house," I answered with a nervous laugh. Charlie pointed to our guests and made a sign as if shooing someone out. How could they not understand?

"Kids always think someone else's house is more fun," one of the visitors said. They did not understand. I told Charlie, "They'll go home soon. When they're gone, you and I will go for ice cream." The great parental cop out: bribery.

"What did you tell him?"

"Oh, I just said we would go to your house another time." I then encouraged Charlie to go play in his room as his patience was clearly (at least to me) wearing wafer thin. Fortunately, the visit ended soon after and everyone was happy. The company believed Charlie had had a wonderful time. Charlie got his ice cream, and I was saved from embarrassment.

When I related this experience to a friend the following day, I intended to make the point that I was placed in the awkward position of having to lie to Charlie as well as to our well-meaning guests. My friend pointed out that I was lucky. A hearing child simply would have blurted out what was on his or her mind. Believing myself to have been saved from utter mortification, I laid to rest any ethical twinges about my lie.

Part of Charlie's campaign to deprive me of any time to myself was his cavalier attitude about going to bed on time. Perhaps he knew that once he fell asleep, I could make as much noise as I liked. Maybe he wanted to keep me from my noise for as long as possible. Whatever the reason, he could think of a long list of activities that demanded his instant attention the minute he saw me sign, "Bedtime." I offer the following as an illustration of a typical night.

It was after 10:00 and Charlie was ready for bed at last. He had come padding into the living room twice now from his bedroom on his little plastic slippered feet. The first time, he looked out the window to verify that my car was still where we had parked it. The second time, he came down the three-foot hall with his hand extended in the sign for *I love you*. His smile was a bit posed, but I have to believe that the sentiment was genuine. Still, the gesture reminded me of the hero in a gothic horror film protecting himself from the vampire with a cross.

On the third trip, Charlie came from his bedroom carrying a book. "Read?" he asked. I still had to sew a button on my coat and struggle through seven sit-ups before going to bed. The spaghetti sauce on the dishes in the sink was crusting to the consistency of cement, but fearful of discouraging Charlie's budding love of literature, I gave in.

We sat on Charlie's bed, cross-legged, facing each other. Charlie held his stuffed dog on his lap, also facing me. Charlie hunched up his shoulders and stared at me intently. I advised him to pay attention to my face, to which he nodded vigorously. He had mastered the delicate balance of looking from the book to my face, but since the pictures in the book were more interesting, the reminder was necessary. Then, I began to read (tell) the story of "Jack and the Beanstalk."

This is Jack.

This is Jack's mother.

This is Jack's house.

Food is all gone. Mama sad. Mama cries. Jack is hungry. He wants to eat.

Mama gives Jack money. Jack goes to the store to buy food.

("*Jack push cart?*" "*Yes, Jack can push the cart.*")

Jack takes the cow to the store.

("*Jack ride cow?*" "*No, Jack walks.*")

This is a man. Jack says hello.

("*Grandpa?*" "*No, it is not Grandpa.*")

Man gives Jack magic beans. Man takes cow.

("*Mistake.*" "*No, not a mistake. Jack trades cow for beans.*")

Jack takes beans home.

("*Eat beans?*" "*No, can't eat magic beans.*")

Jack gives beans to Mama. Mama says, "Bad Jack."

Mama throws beans out window.

(I can see Charlie storing this away for whatever yukky beans his own mother might give him.)

Jack goes to bed.

("Jack mistake." "Yes, little mistake.")

Beans grow.

Jack wakes up. Beans grow to big plant. Like Grandpa's garden.

(The connection between the beans and the plant is lost, but not the reference to Grandpa's tiller, complete with sound effects.)

Jack climbs beanstalk.

("Careful." "Yes, careful.")

Up, up, up.

On top, Jack sees big house.

(A look of incredulity here. We are clearly lost between the big plant and the big house.)

Jack knocks on door.

("Wait?" "Yes, have to wait." We have just agreed one should wait after knocking.)

Jack opens the door. Jack goes in the big house.

See the giant.

("Giant.")

Big man. He says, "Where is Jack?" Jack hides in a cup.

(Charlie seems to pity me for believing in the boy in a cup.)

Giant eats dinner. Jack hides.

("Yukky beans?" "No, giant eats cereal.")

Giant has lots of money.

("Quarters?" "No, gold.")

Giant tired. Giant sleeps.

Jack sees Giant. Jack takes money.

(So end all my attempts to keep Charlie out of my jar of change.)

Jack runs.

("Jack fall?" "No, Jack doesn't fall." This child is a bit over-cautious, I perceive.)

Giant wakes up. Where is Jack?

Giant chases Jack.

Jack climbs down beanstalk.

("Big flower?" "Yes.")

("Careful?" "Yes, careful.")

Giant climbs down beanstalk.

Jack cuts beanstalk. Giant falls.

("Hurt Giant." "Dead Giant.")

("Giant asleep." "Yes, Giant asleep.")

Jack goes to store.

("Push cart." "Yes.")

Takes quarters. Jack buys food. Mama cooks dinner.

Jack is happy. Mama is happy.

("Giant wake up?" "No.")

"Now, Charlie, you read it to me." Charlie flips rapidly through the book to the page where Jack's mother throws the magic beans out of the window. He laboriously turns the book toward me. He also asks me to hold the dog, so we can both see.

"Yukky beans." More page turning.

"Big flower." More page turning.

"Giant asleep." More page turning.

"Giant fall down. Giant asleep."

That was the end of Charlie's story. For all the valuable language we had shared, the written words we noticed and pointed to, and the interaction between mother and child, the magic of "Jack and the Beanstalk" had been reduced to sleeping giants and yukky beans.

8

The problem of what to do with Charlie before and after school persisted all through his first semester. I had found a sitter. (What a find—a baby-sitter who knew sign language. I thought surely my luck had changed when I met her.) Peggy had suggested that Charlie ride the bus to and from her house. That took care of Charlie's quasi-residential status at school, but it did not solve the problem of his long days waiting for me. Nor did it give him what I genuinely believed to be one of his most important needs—socialization with other deaf children. The idea of going to class with deaf children but interacting socially only with hearing children did not seem right somehow. Perhaps because I had just moved to a town where I knew no one and felt my own need for friends with whom I shared common ground did I feel Charlie's need more acutely. That, and the certain knowledge that there was no way I could help Charlie learn to deal with a handicap I did not truly (nor could I ever) understand, helped me forge a solid decision. Charlie would definitely stay in the dormitory next year. On a trial basis. If everything worked out. (Why did my firmly forged decisions always so closely resemble molded Jell-O?)

Having made my decision to let Charlie stay in the dormitory, I was driven by guilt to give him all of my attention that summer. ("Now, if you are going to ask Charlie to stay away from home during the school year, giving you weeknights free, which you do not deserve even though you have not had nor will have a free weekend so long as you live in this town to which you brought Charlie, taking him away from family and friends and all things familiar so you could feel proud of yourself for giving him the best education you could possibly provide, well then, you had better devote this summer to being with Charlie and giving him fun, educational, and language-building experiences he will carry with him for a lifetime.")

Thus, nobly charged, I made plans for a summer jam-packed with motherly self-sacrifice and family fun.

Charlie had wanted a bicycle since he was about two. Every shopping trip included at least one stop in the bicycle department. More correctly, Charlie would manage to slip away from me and find the bicycle department on his own. He would try to pull the bicycles out of their racks or displays and mount them. More than once I got to him in time to hear an annoyed salesperson calling to him, "Little boy. Little boy!" It gave me a certain pleasure to watch their futile attempts to get his attention. If the salesperson seemed unusually nasty, I let him or her try several times to get Charlie to put the bicycle back. Then, before things went too far (that is, before Charlie went too far on the bike), I rescued the situation with a few signs. The salesperson generally retreated, justly chastised.

To start off our memorable summer, I procured a very good second-hand bicycle for Charlie. Of course, I built up to the acquisition for several weeks that spring. "If you do good work at school, Mother will get you a bicycle." "If you go to bed on time, Mother will get you a bicycle." "Only boys who eat all their dinner can have a bicycle." Ad infinitum. I am sure that Charlie was beginning to think that no bicycle, however grand, could be worth all this effort, but he persisted in trying.

The day his bicycle arrived was an exciting one, indeed. Charlie is incapable of suppressing his excitement, and his clapping hands and beaming smile made the occasion a holiday. Charlie, of course, wanted to ride it immediately. I had anticipated this and had planned to take the bicycle to a church parking lot across the street where we could have lots of fun and be undisturbed by cars. I had worked all this out in my mind. A few passes through the parking lot with my steadying hand behind him and Charlie would be riding on his own in an hour or two. I brought a book along, carried under one arm, so that I could read and bask in the sunshine while my son circled contentedly on his new red bicycle. What a picture of familial bliss. What a way to start the Super Summer.

I had never taught anyone to ride a bicycle. I didn't remember anyone ever teaching me to ride a bicycle. It seemed like one of those things that one simply tries a few times and then does. This, however, is not true.

I demonstrated a few of the more basic points for Charlie, such as turning the handlebars, sitting up straight, and applying the brakes. Then, it was his turn to try. He made a rather clumsy mount, with his foot getting stuck slightly on the way over the center bar. No matter. I signed to Charlie to go in a straight line first. "We'll learn turning later," I promised. I held the bar in the back to steady him and motioned for him to go forward. He got his feet mixed up a bit, and I was surprised at how heavy a bicycle is with a forty-five-pound rider wobbling on it. I had to grab the back bar with both hands. It was then I realized that I would have a couple of problems. One was that standing behind Charlie made it impossible to give him directions. Second, when holding onto the bicycle to steady it, it was also impossible to give him directions. In one brief instant of insanity, I tried to steady the bicycle from the front so Charlie could see my face. It was clear that I would not get much reading done that day.

We both worked hard for some time, me moving back and forth from the front where Charlie could see me, to the back where I could hold on. I give Charlie his rightful credit; he made a good many attempts. But, his disappointment was obvious. After eating so many dinners and doing good work at school, and going to bed without a fuss, this was clearly not the reward he had hoped for. Charlie finally gave up, and I was left to push, pull, and drag the bicycle home and up the stairs to our second-floor apartment.

It was a few days before Charlie asked to ride the bicycle again. But, to my great pride (and I admit ashamedly, surprise), he did master the bicycle on his second outing. This time, Charlie suggested that I get him started and then get out of his way. This proved an excellent suggestion, and after a few minor mishaps, he was riding pretty well. Within a few more days, he was an expert. I do wonder, though, why children with perfectly good brakes on their bicycles insist on stopping by dragging their feet on the ground. Perhaps scuffed shoes is some sort of mark of childhood machismo.

I could not have been happier at Charlie's skill on his bicycle. It was one thing that he did according to schedule, just like a hearing child. Of course, as my father reminded me when I mentioned this to him, no one rides a bicycle with his ears. Still, it was another milestone.

There was one small concession we made to Charlie's deafness when he rode his bicycle and that concerned cars. Because we lived in an apartment building situated on a hill, I insisted that Charlie ride in that part of the parking lot which had the least traffic. I also insisted that I stand watch at one end to signal him if a car should approach. Because of the steepness of the hill, it was difficult for the driver of an approaching car to see a child on a bicycle until the car had crested the hill. Then, it could be too late. Also, since Charlie could not hear the car grinding up the hill, he would be much too close to it before he could see it. So, I kept the lookout. It worked well; Charlie watched for my waving arm to signal him to move to the side and stop.

Once, however, there was a breakdown in our system. A car was moving steadily up the hill and I waved frantically at Charlie, who was heading directly into its path. Charlie could not or would not look at me, and a head-on collision seemed imminent. Throwing aside all thought of my own safety, I ran over to Charlie and with one swift move, pushed him off his bicycle onto the ground. The car, which by this time was at the top of the hill, had arrived in time to see only this last moment. Charlie was safely out of the way, although lying on the ground with his red bicycle on top of him. The driver of the car obviously did not understand what he had witnessed and gave me a most disapproving look. Charlie was clearly shocked. His own mother had pushed him off his bicycle, skinning his knee. Never mind that I had saved his life. For an instant, I worried that both Charlie and the driver would come at me at once and throw me to the ground as well. Fortunately, the driver only glared at me as he got out of his car and walked toward the building. Charlie glared at me, too, and began to wail in his most pitiful voice. I looked over to the door of the apartment to see the driver give me one last scowl. I knew where he was going. Straight inside to call the authorities. He probably already had them on the line.

> *"Hello, Child Welfare Department? Yes. I want to report a woman assaulting her child. Yes, her own child. I saw it myself. She shoved him off his bicycle and the bike landed right on top of him. Skinned the kid's knee something awful. Probably blood everywhere by now. If you hurry, you can arrest her now. She's still out there with him. I can hear him screaming all the way in here. Please hurry before she has a chance to do it again."*

I quickly lifted the bicycle off Charlie. I wanted to get him inside and cleaned up before the authorities arrived. My reward for my selfless act was to have to carry both Charlie and the bicycle inside. It took two Band-Aids to cover Charlie's wound, and he kept a respectable distance from me for the rest of the day. I tried to explain that I was only trying to save him from being run over by a car and smashed flat on the ground. A skinned knee was better than a broken head, I reasoned with him. It seemed little consolation as Charlie limped around the rest of the day. I must say, however, that after this incident, Charlie watched for my signals. I'm not sure if it was in cooperation with our system or simply because he did not trust me not to attack him again.

Another part of my Model Family Summer of Fun Program was swimming. It was time to teach Charlie to swim. I freely admit that a small part of my motivation was selfish. I love the water. There is something primordially satisfying about returning to the source of all life, that caldron of surging living molecules from which we all came—the heated, indoor, chlorinated pool. But, good exercise nevertheless. I enrolled Charlie in evening swim lessons. I believed that he would do well in the water. Swimming is, after all, an individual sport, requiring no team members and hence no communication. In my well-meaning, but moronic, way I attempted to make sure that Charlie's communication deficiencies would be taken into consideration when I signed him up for lessons.

"Oh yes, and I should tell you that my son is deaf."

"Yes?"

"Well, you might want to tell the instructor beforehand."

"I'm sure it will be all right. We have had deaf kids before."

("Of course they have, you imbecile. Why must you call attention to it as if it were something people must be warned about. For dramatic effect, I suppose.") I must have expected when I gave this admonition that the young man at the desk would drop his clipboard, and a look of terror would sweep over his face.

> "But, we've never had a (organ music: Ta Da) DEAF student in swim lessons before. Whatever will we do?"
>
> "Now, now. Don't panic."
>
> "But, deaf. You said deaf. Why, he won't be able to hear anything the instructor says."
>
> "She can always show him what he must do."
>
> "Yes, but . . .," the young man is pacing back and forth now. He is twisting the string around his neck from which hangs the ever-present whistle (which Charlie can hear). The fingers around which the string is tightening begin to turn white. "But, what if. . . ."
>
> "Calm yourself. There is no need to panic. I will be there at all times, naturally."
>
> "You will?" A glimmer of hope on that piteously horrified face. "Oh, bless you. What an exemplary mother you are."
>
> "You're right, of course. Now, don't you worry about a thing. I'm sure everything will be all right."

And, it always was all right. Except that I never got to be the exemplary mother. The people I warned about Charlie's deafness usually looked at me with annoyance that I would be so ignorant as to even mention it. I looked like the fool, at least I thought I did.

Swimming lessons went well, despite me. The instructors had no difficulty getting Charlie to do whatever was demonstrated for him to do. He always pays attention to other people better than he does to me. Halfway through the first lesson, I went back from the edge of the pool where I had been standing to join the other parents seated or leaning against the wall. This would be great, I thought.

The lesson was nearly over and the instructors had not asked for my help once. When they announced that the lesson was over, they said it was time to sing a song before going home. "Oh no," I thought, "a song. I distinctly told them . . ." The instructors began to sing "Old McDonald." I knew that one. I ran back to my post at the side of the pool and began signing the song. Charlie looked up at me occasionally. He was more interested in kicking his feet in the water. The other children and their parents had more interest in me. There I stood in front of everyone, fingerspelling "E-I-E-I-O." By the time we got to "Here a quack, there a quack, everywhere a quack-quack" (which I signed "Here a duck, there a duck, everywhere a duck-duck"), the people at the front desk had come to the window to watch. It seemed everyone was watching except Charlie.

When the lesson was truly finished, a few people came up and commented on how interesting it was to watch Charlie and me sign. One of the instructors asked what songs Charlie knew so they could sing one for him next time. I said he knew "Happy Birthday." I thought this a rather strange question. What songs does a deaf kid know? Ha! Then, I stopped my mental ridicule. What songs did he know? I had no idea. He learned songs at school and at church. But, he never signed them for me. When will I ever learn that my condescension always ricochets back to catch me in that hollow space right between the eyes.

In all fairness (to myself) I should add that in one of the later swimming lessons, the teacher admitted that it was sometimes difficult to hold Charlie up in the water and show him how to kick or breathe at the same time. When she let go to tell him something, he sank. I agreed with her that it did make for more of a challenge. Generous me.

It was on one of our frequent outings to the pool that I had one of my worst experiences. Worst, not because I did anything more incredible than I'd done before, but because I did it in front of several people at one time. Signing is a very obvious activity; it tends to attract comments from people who observe Charlie and me doing it. Sometimes we meet people who have a deaf family member, or know some sign language, or are deaf themselves. The latter was the situation on this fateful day. A gentleman came up to me during the rest period and signed "Is he deaf?" I said, "Yes." Then he asked if I were deaf. This time I understood and answered correctly. He had a young girl with him, obviously his daughter and obviously quite accustomed to interpreting for her father, which she did either out of habit or because she had heard how bad I was at reading signs.

The gentleman said his daughter was _____ and made a sign I did not understand. He spelled, "T-W . . .," which I did not catch either, but believed to be the girl's name. She, in the meantime, had taken this opportunity to stop telling me what her father was saying. I smiled politely and said, "His name is Charlie." We chatted for a few minutes. The daughter again told me what her father was saying while I tried not to listen. I am quite sure, however, that I relied as much on what the girl was saying as I did on her father's signs. He was polite enough to go slowly for me.

Rest period was now over and Charlie wanted to go back into the water. I was moving slowly backwards in the way one does when one is trying to break off a conversation when another girl came up and joined us. "My daughter," the gentleman signed. "They are both eleven." "Oh," I said enthusiastically, as if telling him something new, "they are twins."

"Yes," he said with a rather puzzled look. I knew I had done it again. The *T-W. . . .* had been *twin*, not the girl's first name.

"I think Charlie wants to get back in the water," I said with a too light-hearted laugh as I pushed Charlie along toward the far side of the pool. When we got back home, I went directly to the sign dictionary and looked up the sign for *twin*. It was the first sign the man at the pool had made, the one before he spelled out what I thought was his daughter's name. He had told me *twin* twice, and I still hadn't understood it. I wonder if Charlie will ever let me talk to his friends when he grows up.

Charlie graduated from kindergarten right on schedule. For me it was a major miracle. What made it so amazing was that it would have happened at just that time in just that way if Charlie had been a hearing child. As Charlie learned more words, our communication became more effective, more satisfying. We were able to discuss things that we had done the day before or that we would do the day after. Charlie was able to use language in the same way other six-year-olds did. He could complain about his dinner, nag me to buy him a new toy, report on his friend's misbehavior, and swear to his own innocence. Our dialogues remained fairly primitive, but the connection was being made more successfully with each attempt.

This should not be taken to mean that the misunderstandings ceased or that the mistakes or my embarrassment at feeling stupid ended. The most frequent short circuit in our communication became my ignorance of the signs Charlie learned at school. I would ask him to explain, to pantomime, to draw me a picture of what he meant. Our roles reversed, Charlie became the teacher. He taught me many words, and I learned them just as slowly as he had absorbed the first words I taught him.

There were still concepts that eluded Charlie. The first time we took a vacation together, I tried to excite Charlie by telling him where we were going and what we would see. Motel came out, "a place where we pay to sleep and swim." Simple but accurate. I left the delights of stealing those little bitty bars of soap out of my explanation, but he picked it up very quickly once we got there.

What Charlie failed to understand was *vacation*. He understood the term to mean a location. So, each place we stopped, whether to get gas or a sandwich or to check into our motel, he asked, "Where is vacation?" I would answer, "This is vacation."

The farther we went the more confused he became. If the gas station we just left was *vacation*, then where were we going now? And why, he must have wondered, did we drive for two days to come to a gas station? Then, before he could resolve these mysteries, we would stop somewhere else. Again, the question, "Where is vacation?" Again the response, "This is vacation." After looking around at the roadside public lavatory, he probably wished we could return to the gas station.

When at last we reached our true destination, I announced, "This is vacation." Charlie looked around at the resort park to which I had brought him. He scrutinized the rides, the hot dog stands, and all the activity. This did seem better than the other *vacations* we had been through so far. He smiled and said he liked vacation, then he ran off to find the bumper cars. I knew that we had a little gap (read chasm) in our communication, but I decided to let it go. It would be another year before we would go on vacation again, and by then maybe I could make Charlie understand. Better yet, maybe he would learn about it at school.

As Charlie learned more and more words, the difficulty of explaining something not visible right in front of us became easier. Simple sentences were clear—"I want hot dog," "I don't want bath." As more complexity was added to his life, Charlie tried to make his words fit his own mental image of what he wanted to say. But sometimes, his word order was turned around, at least it seemed so to me. This made some ideas difficult to understand. I found that I had to read all his words and then jumble them around for them to make sense to me.

One Saturday we were discussing our afternoon plans over lunch. I needed to wash the car, which was one of Charlie's favorite activities.

"We will eat lunch first, then wash the car," I told Charlie.

"Yes," he signed enthusiastically. He clearly liked the idea. "Wash car first lunch."

"No," I corrected, "we eat lunch first, then wash the car."

"Yes," Charlie agreed, "wash car first lunch."

"We will eat first," I signed emphatically. "If you think I'm

139

going to just go off and leave this barbeque beef sandwich, which I starved all week to save up the calories for, then you can just reconsider." This last part was not signed. As slowly as I signed, it would have lost most of its impact. However, Charlie knew my fuse had been touched off, and he waited patiently until I finished. His look of kind tolerance was maddening.

"Okay," he signed, "wash car first lunch."

"Fine," I said. Why go through this anymore when he was clearly so agreeable. He was, after all, eating his lunch and making none of his customary preparations (putting as many toy cars in his pockets as they could hold) to leave the house.

Why I wondered, did he insist on saying it backwards when he seemed to understand what I meant? I kept going over the phrase in my mind, "Wash car first lunch." Some lightning bolt of insight told me to try a pause, "Wash car, first lunch." It worked. Charlie had me again. But why didn't he use the proper word order? Why wasn't he speaking English? The answer came with much reflection, much later.

Charlie doesn't speak English because he doesn't really know English. His first language is one of gestures. As Charlie is exposed more and more to deaf adults, in school and through outside activities, he is learning to use American Sign Language (ASL). While linguists may debate the question, I will boldly assert that ASL is a different language from English. ASL differs from English in several ways, including word order and its use of one or two signs for a concept that requires several words in English. ASL eliminates the use of such grammatical devices as articles, tense endings, and, sometimes, plurals except when needed for clarification.

ASL is a language rich in visual description, but ASL is not English. How does one who does not use conversational English learn to read English? Signed English was created to solve this problem. Signed English takes the signs of ASL and uses them in English word order. In Signed English, every jot and tittle of the English phrase is signed, including the tense of the verbs. Signed English is used to teach reading to deaf children, but it is not seen much in their casual sign conversations. Will Charlie's use of ASL prove to be a problem in teaching him to read? I think not. Most of us can use better English than we do in our daily conversations. We read at a more sophisticated level than we speak. My hope is that Charlie will learn to move freely between Signed English and ASL and to use each at its appropriate time.

Of all the good things that happened as Charlie grew, the most useful was, of course, communication. The most exciting was his enjoyment of music. The first time I saw him turn on my tape player and lay his ear down on the speaker, I stood motionless. He swayed slightly with the beat. I had a small portable tape player, so I picked it up and let Charlie hold it to his ear. I started to dance, and he moved with me. He did not miss a beat. He had not displayed the same interest in the car radio or in music on television. This was probably because he couldn't feel the vibrations as intensely as he could by holding the tape player speaker directly on his ear. I did not know what he heard, but we danced, we bopped, we moved. My neighbors probably thought Charlie was climbing on the furniture when I shouted, "Get down, Charlie." He liked the music. It made him feel good and it made him want to dance. Is music more than this to anyone?

How far we have come from that morning in the doctor's office. Looking out of the window with my baby in my arms seems like another lifetime ago. Some of the hurt remains. How can it ever go away?

But look where we are now. Charlie is living in the dormitory at school. Few people understand that decision, except other parents of deaf children. That's all right. I've learned to ignore that look I sometimes get when I tell people that Charlie stays in the dormitory during the school week. I no longer squirm at the "I wouldn't let my child go away to school," that lurks behind every "Well, it's your decision." I find that avoiding the whole discussion works best. Charlie's hearing playmates are not so diplomatic.

141

"Where's Charlie?"

"He's at school."

"He goes to school at night?"

"No, he stays in the dormitory at his school. He'll be home Friday and you can play then."

"You mean he doesn't come home from school at night?"

"Not during the week, no."

"Wow. Does he have to sleep at his desk?"

"Oh no. He has a bed and everything."

I am not prepared to discuss the benefits of residential education at this time. I don't have that wonderful perspective of time, yet. I believe it is the right decision. Charlie's behavior and progress tell me it is right. Winston Churchill went away to boarding school when he was only five, and he turned out all right. When Charlie learns to read well enough, I plan to get a TDD. (A telecommunications device for the deaf; it's like a small typewriter that connects to the telephone. Two people carry on a conversation by typing messages back and forth.) I won't miss him so much when I'm able to call him. I wonder if he'll call me.

I'm still amazed at how far we have come with communication. Charlie and I now carry on quite proper conversations. It is still a wonder to me, after struggling for so long, to be able to ask for and receive information from Charlie.

More aware of the world around him, Charlie wants everything explained to him. If he sees a car stopped by the side of the road, he says, "What happened?" I usually make something up if it is not evident. So far, it has worked well, but I think one day soon he will question "broken car" as the explanation for all nonmoving vehicles. Charlie also wants to know what is happening when he watches television. If I can just fake it until he learns to read the captions for himself, I'll be all right.

Charlie is learning to read. Slow going, now, but how fast the learning will come when he masters that. He wants to know what everything says from street signs to package labels. Try fingerspelling *monosodium glutamate*. Sitting down with him and a book and watching him sign each word as I point to it is thrilling beyond description.

Charlie's speech is still quite unintelligible for all but those closest to him. He needs to be reminded to use his voice. Without a sign, I even fail to understand certain vocal attempts.

There is no way for me to simulate or understand Charlie's almost complete absence of sound from birth. It is entirely impossible to imagine the thought processes of one with so little language. My conscious memory goes back only as far as my language. We all remember images, of course. But, try to remember some incident without letting your mind use any words. It is not possible to do. And yet, Charlie thinks, understands, and remembers things with only minimal language and without the sound of one single word in his brain.

I don't understand that process, and that mystery is part of the gulf between us. I cannot eradicate language from my mind to try to understand how Charlie thinks, as I might try to blindfold myself for a day if he were blind. The miracle is that he does think and imagine and create and reason and learn. Maybe one day he'll explain it to me. For now, I content myself with the miracle.

I do know that Charlie speaks to me. He always has. With his hands, with his face, with his eyes, with his whole body, he speaks to me. What energetic conversations we have. What glorious communication lies ahead, now that I have finally learned to understand him.

Related books of interest

Deaf Like Me, by Thomas S. Spradley & James P. Spradley
Broken Ears, Wounded Hearts, by George A. Harris
A Hug Just Isn't Enough, by Caren Ferris

For more information on these books, plus sign language and other deafness-related publications, write for a free catalog.

Gallaudet College Press
800 Florida Avenue NE
Washington, DC 20002

DATE DUE

F			
01.18.89			
MAY 10 '89			

DEMCO NO. 38-298